The
After-Dinner Joke
and
Three More Sleepless Nights

Caryl Churchill

◆

Edited by Lib Taylor

Series Editor: Judith Baxter

The publishers would like to thank Nicholas McGuinn and
Jane Ogborn for their help as consulting editors for the series.

14979

AYLESBURY COLLEGE

822·91
CHU

LIBRARY

Published by the Press Syndicate of the University of Cambridge
The Pitt Building, Trumpington Street, Cambridge CB2 1RP
40 West 20th Street, New York, NY 10011-4211, USA
10 Stamford Road, Oakleigh, Melbourne 3166, Australia

This edition of *Three More Sleepless Nights* and *The After-Dinner Joke*
is published by arrangement with Nick Hern Books Ltd. The texts were
first published in *Shorts*, a volume of ten short plays by Caryl Churchill.
Text © Caryl Churchill 1990
Introduction © Caryl Churchill 1995
Resource notes © Cambridge University Press 1995
Back cover picture: copyright Val Rylands

First published 1995

Printed and bound by Scotprint Ltd, Musselburgh, Scotland

A catalogue record for this book is available from the British Library

ISBN 0 521 48571 1 paperback

Prepared for publication by Stenton Associates

CONTENTS

──────────────────── ◆ ────────────────────

CAMBRIDGE LITERATURE

This edition of Caryl Churchill's two plays is part of the Cambridge Literature series, and has been specially prepared for students in schools and colleges who are studying the book as part of their English course.

This study edition invites you to think about what happens when you read the plays. It suggests that you are not passively responding to words on the page which have only one agreed interpretation, but that you are actively exploring and making new sense of what you read and act out. Your 'reading' will partly stem from you as an individual, from your own experiences and point of view, and to this extent your interpretation will be distinctively your own. But your reading will also stem from the fact that you belong to a culture and a community, rooted in a particular time and place. So, your understanding may have much in common with that of others in your class or study group.

There is a parallel between the way you read the plays and the way they were written. The Resource Notes at the back are devised to help you to investigate the complex nature of the writing and dramatisation process. This begins with the playwright's first, tentative ideas and sources of inspiration, moves through to the stages of writing, publication and stage production, and ends with the play's reception by the audience, reviewers, critics and students. So the general approach to study focuses on five key questions:

Who has written these plays and why?

What type of plays are these?

How were these plays produced?

How do the plays present their subjects?

Who reads/watches these plays? How do they interpret them?

The Resource Notes encourage you to take an active and imaginative approach to studying the plays both in and out of the classroom. As well as providing you with information about many aspects of the plays they offer a wide choice of activities to work on individually, or in groups. Above all, they give you the chance to explore the plays in a variety of ways: as a reader, an actor, a researcher, a critic, and a writer.

Judith Baxter

INTRODUCTION

by Caryl Churchill

The After-Dinner Joke

The After-Dinner Joke was written for television in response
to Margaret Matheson, who was producing *Play for Today*,
saying she wanted plays about public rather than domestic
subjects, and asking if I'd think about charities. I did a certain
amount of research, contacting various charities and talking to
people who had been abroad on their behalf. I think at the time
War on Want was the charity most explicitly aware of the
political issues; now it's more generally acknowledged. But
charities are not supposed to get political or they cease legally
to be able to operate as charities, so they can't go too far in
that direction.

Though I'd already done some television plays I'd mostly
written for the theatre, so I was thinking what it was about TV
as a medium that I most enjoyed. I found it was two extremes
– very naturalistic pieces like Roland Joffe's *Scroungers*, or very
non-naturalistic ones like *Monty Python's Flying Circus*. It was
this fast-moving style of sketches and cartoons I fancied for the
charities play. It was good for dealing with ideas as well as
incidents and for leaping from place to place, and gave the
whole thing an energy and lightness that made it easier to take
on the seriousness of the subject.

The title comes from an Oxfam publication, *The After
Dinner Joke Book*, which was a collection of jokes told by
famous people in speeches after large public dinners.

Three More Sleepless Nights

Three More Sleepless Nights was the next play I wrote after *Cloud Nine*. *Cloud Nine* had been written after a period of research with Joint Stock Theatre Group and with the pressure of knowing the tour was booked before the play was written. *Three More Sleepless Nights* was a play I wrote on the spur of the moment without knowing where it would be done. It was directed by Les Waters, who had been the assistant director of *Cloud Nine*, at the Soho Poly Theatre, a theatre that did short new plays at lunch time.

I seem to remember one of the ideas behind the play was of people trying to change but finding it almost impossible when their social circumstances haven't changed. But I don't think that's what's most apparent about it. The first two scenes are different kinds of quarrel. In the first, the two people talk all the time and often both at once. In the second, the two people hardly say anything and there are long silences. The silences should be very long – my memory is that that scene used to last seventeen minutes, though I could be wrong.

I wondered about the best way of writing down the over-lapping dialogue in the first scene and decided it would be clearest in two columns, but that I wanted to indicate exactly where in one person's speech the other person started talking. I decided to indicate it with / , I think because in a book I'd read with some documentary excerpts of taped talk it had been done that way and seemed clear. A couple of years later I wrote a play called *Top Girls* where six people were having dinner together and I decided they should have overlapping conversations. Six columns wasn't practical on a page, and anyway all six weren't talking at once, but I did keep the use of / for showing where the different voices came in, and it's a device I've often used since.

June 1994

The
After-Dinner Joke

List of characters in order of appearance

Selby, a young woman

Price, an old man

Popstar, a man of maybe 30

Mayor, a man of at least 45

Celebrity, a woman, any age

3 councillors, men or women, any age

3+ fasters, men or women, fairly young

Children, various

3+ record breakers, various

Son, 9 to 11 years old

Mum, 30+

Bruce Wingfield, a middle-aged man

Thief, a young man

Baby

Customer, a man, any age

Licensee, a man, any age

Man with jubilee mug, middle-aged

Collector, a young man

Woman with shoe, any age

Assistant, a woman, any age

Man with camera, or woman

Woman with catalogue, over 50

Old lady

Buyer, needn't be a man

Salesman, likely to be a man

Oil sheikh, any age

Wives, any age

Bodyguards, young enough to look strong

Knitted-hat lady, at least 45

Dent, about 45

Woman, probably middle-aged

Tea managing director, about 60

Sir Arthur, about 60

Mother, young

Baby

Man, about 30

Girl, 20s

Cowboys, various

Child, any

American patient, 50 to 60 years old

Arab gardener, a man, any age

Villain, a man, any age

Peasant, a man, any age

Minister, not under 40

Passenger, a man, 45 to 60 years old

Girl, 20s

Guerrilla, a man, any age except old

Journalist, man or woman, any age

Businessmen, mainly middle-aged

Peasants, men or women, any age

The only parts of any size are Selby, Price, Mayor, Dent. The others can be doubled, trebled, quadrupled …

The After-Dinner Joke was first transmitted on BBC1 on 14 February 1978, directed by Colin Bucksey. The cast was as follows:

Selby,   Paula Wilcox
Price,   Richard Vernon
Dent,   Clive Merrison
Mayor,   Derek Smith
Bruce Wingfield,   Ben Aris
Passenger,   Philip Sayer
Patient,   Hal Galili
Girl,   Heather Wright
Journalist,   Tom Georgeson
Thief,   George Innes
Minister,   James Bree
Celebrity,   Sheila Brennan
Knitted-hat lady,   Patricia Lawrence
Mum,   Sandy Ratcliff
Upper-class woman,   Julia McCarthy
Woman with catalogue,   Stella Moray
Popstar,   Peter Blake
Tea manager,   Raymond Francis
Collector,   Lee Walker
Man in pub,   Richard Aylen
Merchant,   Saeed Jaffrey
Sheikh,   Ishaq Bux
Cowboy,   Luke Hanson

One

[PRICE *and* SELBY.]

[PRICE *is sitting behind a large desk;* SELBY *is standing in front of it.*]

PRICE Do I understand you're resigning, Miss Selby?

SELBY I want to do good, Mr Price.

PRICE And you think that being personal secretary to my sales manager isn't doing good?

SELBY No, sir. 5

PRICE Perhaps you think my sales manager isn't doing good?

SELBY It's just that I –

PRICE Perhaps you think the whole of Price's Bedding isn't doing good? 10

SELBY It's not, no.

PRICE And you think my department store doesn't do good?

SELBY No, it doesn't.

PRICE And I suppose my estate agents don't do good? 15

SELBY No.

PRICE And my launderettes and my chinese restaurants and my novelty factory making fireworks and crackers?

SELBY No.

PRICE I give employment. I provide services. I pay taxes. I 20
make profits.

SELBY Children are dying, sir.

PRICE I see.

SELBY The cost of a six-foot Weldorm with Slumberland mattress and headboard would buy a pump for a well 25
and a camel cart and a –

PRICE Miss Selby, are you a Christian?

SELBY Not any more. But I feel just as guilty as if I was. And so should you.

PRICE Well done, Miss Selby, well done. When I was a   30
young man and bought a penny doughnut for my tea, I
always put a penny in the lifeboat stocking. And as I
built up from my first little shop, my great joy has
always been that I have given more and more to
charity.   35

[*He gets out a bottle of whisky and two glasses and pours drinks as he talks.*]

I am on the boards of five charities. Two great
charities I founded myself. And I will be happy to go
on paying your salary, Miss Selby, while you work full
time as one of our campaign organisers raising funds
in towns throughout the country. Your health.   40

SELBY I don't usually like to drink, sir, because the cost of
one glass of whisky would buy thirty trees to prevent
soil erosion.

PRICE You can stop feeling guilty about world poverty,
Miss Selby. You've started doing something about it.   45

SELBY Cheers.

[*She knocks back her drink.*]

Two

[*A* POPSTAR.]

POPSTAR I said gimme
I said gimme what I need I said gimme
I said
gimme gimme gimme gimme gimme gimme
gimme gimme gimme   5
[*Cheers and screams.*]

Now that song is from two years back and I still sing it
because it still sells but it's not true now I've
discovered Jesus. I know now how to get what I want.
I do the opposite. Yes, that's right. God moves in these
mysterious ways. How you get what you want is you   10
give. If you give you're needed. If you're needed you're
loved. You need to be needed. You need to be loved.
That's what you're after. That's what I'm after.
Gimme love. Now if you give, the people you give to
are going to love you. Jesus Christ is going to love you. 15
And I am going to love you.

    [*Cheers and screams.*]

Three

[SELBY *and the* MAYOR.]

[*A large wall-map of the town.*]

SELBY What I want to know, Mr Mayor, is where in your
town the people with money are, so I can get it off
them.

MAYOR You won't find it easy. They're all conservatives
and won't play golf with me.   5

SELBY Where do they live?

MAYOR Up here on the hill.

SELBY And down here?

MAYOR Between the high street and the canal is what we
call the old town.   10

SELBY The slums.

MAYOR The redevelopment area.

SELBY I just don't want to waste any leaflets. If you give
me the population and housing statistics I can rule out
the areas with multi-occupation.   15

MAYOR Just because the conservatives have more money that's no reason to think we in the labour movement aren't as generous as anyone else. Just because Ted Heath° conducts Christmas carols –

SELBY No, I didn't mean to imply –   20

MAYOR and Margaret Thatcher° supports Help the Aged and Prince Charles makes a jubilee° appeal –

SELBY No, of course –

MAYOR Everyone thinks they're so kindhearted, and I'm every bit as kindhearted as they are, just because   25
they're crowned heads, I'd be generous if I had a palace full of royal heritage and my mug on mugs, and a certain conservative councillor I can name keeps his wife on such a tight allowance she had to ask for an extra half-p when the postage went up so she could   30
write to her lover –

SELBY No politics, please.

MAYOR I beg your pardon?

SELBY A charity is by definition nonpolitical. Politics is by definition uncharitable.   35

MAYOR But this poor lady is kept on a shoestring and charity begins at home, and this conservative councillor –

SELBY The royal family takes part in charity, so that just shows. Royalty is charitable. Royalty is nonpolitical.   40
Therefore charity is nonpolitical.

MAYOR If I could take that again slowly. Royalty is charitable. Charity is nonpolitical. Therefore royalty is nonpolitical.

SELBY Do you doubt that?   45

MAYOR In a certain light everything is political.

SELBY There's nothing political at all about royalty.

MAYOR There's something political about everything.

SELBY Everything except royalty. And charities. What's political about royalty? Horses? Badminton horse   50

14

trials, polo at Windsor, racing at Epsom? Or cars?
Princess Anne breaking the speed limit? A jubilee
parade of antique Rolls Royces? You're going to try
and tell me that a queen and dukes and an honours list
and men on the moor banging away at grouse and   55
thousands of pounds' worth of shares that are
undisclosed have something to do with politics, but
that only goes to show how wrong you are.

MAYOR Are you interested in snakes at all?

SELBY No, not at all. I'm only interested in not wasting   60
my valuable leaflets paid for by people who want to
think every penny goes into powdered milk and
blankets, silly buggers, how do they think they'd know
about us if we didn't pay for advertising? No, I don't
mean they're silly buggers, they're wonderful   65
warmhearted folk, and I'm not wasting their valuable
leaflets on unemployed nerks who won't give a good
return for time and motion spent.

MAYOR That's a pity, because snakes are completely
nonpolitical and I have a very interesting collection of   70
pythons and boa constrictors and –

SELBY You get the odd old-age pensioner with pennies in
the teapot and it's the thought that counts but widows'
mites don't pay for wellbores, and I'm sure as a
supporter of our charity you'd agree –   75

MAYOR I don't give that for your charity, to be honest. I'm
only interested in my snakes. The largest python is
nearly fifteen feet long. I sometimes go out at night in
the springtime with a large sack and I have him on a
special lead with a harness I've made and I creep up to   80
this field with all the lambs and I open the sack and –

Four

[*A* CELEBRITY.]

CELEBRITY I've been asked to launch this charity campaign
because I'm a local celebrity and everyone will think
that if they give something they'll be celebrities too. It's
only charity organisers who've ever actually called me
a celebrity, which certainly isn't the only reason I   5
support charities but because of their wonderful work
with the starving millions. Now I write a cookery
column and how lucky we are to have delicious dishes
even at today's prices compared to the starving
millions who have less calories in one day than you   10
have for breakfast, unless you're one of those sillies
who goes without breakfast. Always always have a
cooked breakfast, even if you're on a diet, because –
But anyway in Ethiopia not so long ago people were
dying by the roadside and in Bangladesh many people   15
are lucky if they have a bowl of rice and vegetables at
a feeding station, and lucky they are, because I have a
recipe this week for courgettes au gratin with saffron
rice which you just crisp up under the grill and – as I
was saying these poor people may have nothing in the   20
larder but a little pile of flour and a few beans and,
however good the recipe, ingredients do make all the
difference, so always use the best butter, free-range
eggs, double cream, because no one in the Third World
is actually going to benefit by you eating margarine,   25
the only thing of course is watch the cholesterol. But if
you feel like spoiling yourself, and in these days of
inflation luxuries have actually gone up less than
necessities so it's economic sense to live well if you can,

I have a recipe here where you wrap the smoked   30
salmon round the –

Five

[*Three* COUNCILLORS *are sitting in a sideshow, with the labels* LIB, LAB, CON, *and people are paying 50p to throw pies at them. Splat. A custard pie is thrown in the face of a* COUNCILLOR. *They are keeping cheerful. Pies keep coming.*]

VOICES [*In the crowd*]. Nice to see them working together
for once.

It's what this country needs to set it on its feet.

Daddy, what's lib lab con?

Well sweetheart, the Labour Party and the Liberal   5
Party got together and that's known as the lib-lab* con.

Don't they mind?

I expect they like the attention.
    [*Splat, splat.*]

Six

[*The* MAYOR.]

MAYOR – a large lump in the python which is the lamb it
has swallowed whole, it's amazing how their throats
open and their scales spread, and the python will lie
still for a long time while the creature is gradually
digested and not require any food for several weeks.   5

17

Seven

[*More sideshows.*]

[*A sponsored fast.*]

[*Some of the group are exhausted, others are squabbling.*]

1   Sugar's cheating.
2   No, it's not.
1   Yes it is, we said liquids but no milk and sugar.
2   Then why's it all right for you to drink orange juice?
3   I've lost five pounds but I bet I put it all on again.   5
    [*A sponsored silence.*]
    [*A group of children, all except one near bursting point from keeping quiet. Finally one starts to giggle, they all start, except the one, who goes on sitting silently.*]
    [*Sponsored record breakers.*]
    [*Various activities; e.g., a girl standing on her head, a boy playing a comb and tissue paper, a man eating doughnuts.*]

Eight

[*A* SON *and his* MUM.]

SON I don't want to go on the sponsored walk.
MUM You got all those names.
SON I got a tummy-ache.
MUM How much you got a mile if you add it all up?
SON Eighty p.   5
MUM If you walk ten miles that's eight pounds.

18

SON Why can't they just give me the money?

MUM You have to earn it. People won't give money for nothing.

SON It doesn't do them any good if I walk does it? 10

MUM It's good for you.

SON I got a tummy-ache.

MUM It's fresh air.

SON If they want to give the money, I don't see why they can't just give it, I don't see why I have to walk round 15 and round the park all afternoon, I want to play football and watch telly, why can't they sponsor me to watch telly, I'd do that for hours, they'd get far more out of me, I don't see how it's going to help some hungry person in Africa if I walk round and round the 20 park all afternoon with a tummy-ache and get blisters and –

MUM All right, I'll buy you training shoes, now stop going on.

SON Will you, Mum? Now? Now will you? For this 25 afternoon?

MUM All right, I said I will, now give over.

SON They're really good, Mum, everyone's got them and they're only seven ninety-five and I'll walk ten miles in them easy, well nine or ten. 30

Nine

[*The* MAYOR.]

MAYOR Snakes aren't slimy. People think they are. They don't feel like frogs. They're really very pleasant to the touch.

Ten

[SELBY *and* BRUCE WINGFIELD.]

[BRUCE *is practising golf shots with a fixed ball on his lawn.*]

BRUCE I already give a great deal to charity.

SELBY Which charities do you give to?

BRUCE There's one to support Eton College and one to support the London Clinic and one –

SELBY But those are charities that help the rich. I thought   5
charities had to help the poor.

BRUCE Are you getting political?

SELBY No no no.

BRUCE They are very old, established charities set up to
provide education and hospital care.   10

SELBY But the government provides those nowadays.

BRUCE The government also provides foreign aid.

SELBY Ah but charities though small go direct to the
people, bypassing all governments whatever their
politics, and set up different schemes the government   15
hasn't covered and –

BRUCE Exactly, and I've found something the government
hasn't covered and I'm setting up a charity to benefit
company directors called Bruce Wingfield, five foot
ten, brown hair, living in Englefield Avenue, and   20
playing golf.

SELBY Would you be a beneficiary of this charity?

BRUCE As it happens, yes, I would.

SELBY You can't do that. It has to be a broader category.
The charity commissioners would never allow it.   25

BRUCE Are you quite sure?

SELBY Almost.

BRUCE Perhaps if I make it company directors called
  Bruce, five foot ten *to eleven*, brown *or mousy* hair,
  living in Englefield Avenue *or Gardens*. And playing   30
  golf.
SELBY You've already got a two-car garage.
BRUCE Are you getting political?
SELBY No no no no no, I'm not getting political, no –

Eleven

[*The* COUNCILLORS; *a* THIEF.]

[*Splat. Another pie. The* COUNCILLORS *are trying to look as
if they're still enjoying it.*]

[*In the crowd, a* THIEF *picks a pocket.*]

Twelve

[*A* MUM *and her* BABY.]

MUM Eat up for Mummy.
BABY No.
MUM Just a spoonful for Mummy.
BABY No.
MUM Spoonful for Daddy.   5
BABY No.
MUM Spoonful for Nan.
BABY No.
MUM Spoonful for Batman.
  [*The* BABY *opens his mouth and has some. Then spits it
  out.*]

Batman's going to be very cross with you. Batman   10
won't let you be Robin. Batman's going to give you to
the Joker and he'll put you in a machine that'll take all
your brains away and you'll be a vegetable, you'll be a
plate of gooey green spinach yourself.

[*MUM calms herself and starts again.*]

Open your mouth. Doggy's going to get it. Doggy   15
wants your dindin. Open quick. Mummy give dindin
to doggy. Look there's thousands of people would like
this dinner, right? There's millions of Indians want this
dinner. This is your last chance, right? Right. I'm
sending it to India. Everything. Yes even your sweeties,   20
bad boys don't get sweeties.

[*MUM puts the food from the table and fridge into a
carrier bag.*]

Sweeties go to India, eggies go to India, crispy cod fries
go to India, crinkle cut chips go to India, prawn curry
goes to India, raspberry ripple ice cream goes to India,
fizzy orange goes to India, you sodding go to India.   25

[*MUM puts the bag over the BABY's head.*]

Thirteen

[SELBY, *a* CUSTOMER *and a* LICENSEE.]

SELBY Twenty pence would vaccinate a child against
measles, fifty pence would buy eighty trees to prevent
soil erosion, one pound would buy eight feet of
waterpipe, five pounds would buy a pig.

[*An off-licence.*]

CUSTOMER Bottle of whisky, please.   5

LICENSEE Here you are, sir.

[*The LICENSEE gives the CUSTOMER a pig.*]

Fourteen

[*Stock film of a sponsored walk.*]

Fifteen

[*The* MAYOR *and* SELBY.]

MAYOR I challenge you to tell me something apart from
my snakes that is not political.
SELBY Anything. Just look about you. Say – anything.
MAYOR Say something.
SELBY House. No, wait a minute, not a house. Car. No, 5
not a car. Tree. Tree.
MAYOR Tree. Timber. Price of. Building industry. Need I
say more?
SELBY Rain.
MAYOR Rain. Leaks. Section 99 of the Public Health Act 10
calling for repairs to substandard housing. The number
of prosecutions in this town last year –
SELBY Fish. No no no, not fish. Not fish. Not cow. Haha,
butter mountain. No farm animals. Wildebeest.
MAYOR A wildebeest is a South African animal. 15
SELBY Not a wildebeest, no, I didn't say wildebeest. I said
butterfly. That's it, butterfly. Butterfly, summer day,
blue sky, flowers, long grass, strolling through the long
grass with a nice bloke and finding a place to sit down
among all the flowers and butterflies. 20

Sixteen

[*A* MAN *with a jubilee mug and a* COLLECTOR *with long hair.*]

MAN Give money to blacks?

COLLECTOR Yeh well I mean like they're dying man.

MAN If I give them money they'll recover and land on the Sussex coast at dead of night and come and live next door.   5

COLLECTOR No, if you don't give they'll get angry and all the ones that haven't died will get the atom bomb from Russia and drop it on you.

MAN Really?

COLLECTOR Yeh.   10

MAN What if I do give then?

COLLECTOR Then they'll be very grateful and stay where they belong and take O level English Literature and buy all our exports and wish they were still in the Empire and remember you in their prayers and think   15 you're great, man.

MAN Really?

COLLECTOR Yeh.

MAN Oh all right, here you are.
      [*He puts money in the collecting-box.*]

Seventeen

[*The* MAYOR.]

MAYOR Butterfly. Not so many about. Industrial pollution.

Eighteen

[*A* WOMAN *with a shoe, and an* ASSISTANT.]

WOMAN Have you got these in a five?
ASSISTANT Here you are.
    [*She drags out a fishing boat.*]

Nineteen

[*A* MAN *with a camera; a* THIEF.]

[*The* MAN *is taking pictures of the sponsored record breakers. He puts the camera down on a seat beside him for a moment. The* THIEF *takes it.*]

Twenty

[*A* WOMAN *with a catalogue,* SELBY *and an* OLD LADY.]

WOMAN We've adopted a granny.
SELBY That's wonderful.
WOMAN We had a catalogue from your company and we
    chose one. We'll get a grandpa next year to match.
SELBY Which one did you choose?   5
    [*The* WOMAN *shows the photographs in the catalogue.*]
WOMAN We asked for this one which was advertised, it
    says ninety-two and never a day of ill health, always
    cheerful – well, compared to my mother, I can tell
    you. But she'd already gone so they sent us another

model, she's eighty-one and has suffered from leprosy   10
for many years so that she has no fingers, but you
can't catch it at this distance, and she sends us the
nicest letters telling us how grateful she is and how
wonderful we are, which is more than my mother ever
did.   15

SELBY Is your mother dead?

WOMAN Oh no, I don't think so. We keep her in the
corner. You don't want to get her noticing, you don't
want to set her off talking, she's not at all a nice old
lady.   20

    [*SELBY reaches out to touch the OLD LADY's shoulder.
The OLD LADY bites her hand.*]

Twenty-one

[*The* COUNCILLORS; SELBY.]

[*The* COUNCILLORS *are finishing cleaning themselves up.*]

LIB We made nearly fifty pounds.

CON I'd rather have written a cheque for fifty pounds.

LAB Most of the pies were thrown at me.

CON Yes, I reckon it's the equivalent of a 20 per cent
swing.   5

LAB They naturally throw pies at the one in power. It
shows respect.

LIB They threw quite a lot at me.

CON Never had so much notice taken of you.

LAB It's by association with me.   10

LIB Oh look. There's one pie left.

    [*LIB edges towards the pie.*]

LAB No, Harry.

CON Not when we've just got washed.

LAB We are on the same side.
CON I was hoping you'd join me for dinner. 15
[*SELBY comes in.*]
SELBY I'd just like to thank you all so much for –
[*Splat: Pie in SELBY's face.*]

Twenty-two

[*The* THIEF *climbs in through a window.*]

Twenty-three

[SELBY *and the* MAYOR.]

SELBY Sunset.
MAYOR Sunset. Romance.
SELBY Romance, there you are.
MAYOR Sunset. Romance. Marriage. Housework. Wages
for Housework. We're getting into a whole area here – 5
SELBY Don't bother.
MAYOR Sex Discrimination Act. Equal pay.
SELBY I didn't mean sunset. Not sun*set*. Sunrise.
MAYOR Sun*rise*?
SELBY Yes. 10
MAYOR Rising sun?
SELBY That's right.
MAYOR Land of the rising sun? Japan? Rate of growth?
SELBY Not so much sun*rise*. Just sun.
MAYOR *Sun*. Newspaper. 15
SELBY No no, sun in the sky.
MAYOR Sun.
SELBY Sun.

Twenty-four

[*A* BUYER *and a* CAR SALESMAN.]

BUYER When can I have delivery of this model?
SALESMAN Right away sir.
    [*Enter fifty calves.*]

Twenty-five

[*The* POPSTAR *and* SELBY.]

[*They are sharing a joint in the front of the* POPSTAR*'s parked car, while young girls swarm at the windows and on the bonnet.*]

POPSTAR I really fancy girls about ten or twelve years old and they besiege me, they get in the car somehow – I expect there's one in the back now but I can't be bothered to turn round – I book into a hotel room and there's one waiting, but I reckon Jesus understands   5 that because all you need is love isn't it, or it used to be a few years back, but now I find I need fast cars as well.
SELBY I do want to be liked. You're right there. It's not a good feeling that a whole lot of people round the   10 world might be hating you. When I started this job, it was such a relief. But now unless I raise more and more each time I feel as bad as before I started. I don't know if this appeal's done any good.
POPSTAR It can't do my sales any harm. Whether it does   15 any good to – what is it this time? Starving

28

Bangladeshis it was a few years back, and Ethiopia's
not in the charts now but these things are always with
us, and I really do envy your job, it's the only thing I'd
like to do except be a really great rock star. I mean   20
love and starvation are two of the basics. And fast cars.

Twenty-six

[*An* OIL SHEIKH, *his* VEILED WIVES *and their*
BODYGUARDS.]

[*Marks and Spencer's. The* WIVES *are picking up armfuls of
clothes and giving them to the* BODYGUARDS, *who are
holding piles of clothes.*]

SHEIKH [*in Arabic*] Stop.
      [*They stop.*]
      [*In English*] This is a waste of time. I will buy
      everything. All the sweaters. All the shirts. All the
      underwear. The whole shop. All the shop assistants.
      The whole building.   5
      [*SELBY and the MAYOR.*]
MAYOR An Arab oil sheikh has just bought Marks and
      Spencer's. He's having it taken down and shipped
      brick by brick back to the desert.
SELBY Quick, he might give something.
MAYOR I wonder if he'd like to take the town hall. I could   10
      start collecting scorpions.
      [*The SHEIKH and SELBY.*]
      [*The SHEIKH takes bundles of notes from under his robe
      and gives them to SELBY.*]
SHEIKH For the poor English.
      [*A VOICE over stills.*]

VOICE Camels have been replaced by Cadillacs in Kuwait
which brings smiles to the inhabitants of Kensington
and Chelsea as they receive their first gifts of discarded   15
camels.
    [*A still of English people with a camel.*]
Strikers at a midland car factory who would like to be
adopted by an Arab family.
    [*A still of strikers.*]
Bales of clothing have been opened and distributed,
bringing delight to this old Englishman.   20
    [*A rapid series of stills of an old Englishman taking off
    his clothes and struggling into Arab robes.*]

Twenty-seven

[PRICE *and* SELBY.]

PRICE Well done, Miss Selby, well done. That's the largest
sum ever collected in one town and makes you
regional organiser of the year with your picture in our
newsletter. I'd like you to attend my next business
lunch where I persuade as many businessmen as   5
possible to involve their companies in charity work
and I'd like you to learn all about tax concessions so
you can talk to them. And then I'd like to promote you
to the publicity department of our central office.

Twenty-eight

[*A* LADY *in a knitted hat;* DENT.]

DENT [*voice*] A message from the publicity department.
LADY People think charities are just ladies in knitted hats
with nothing better to do, very amateurish and
muddled but full of warmth and compassion. Well I
work for this charity and that is exactly what I'm like   5
but the charity itself is extremely businesslike and
professional and commercial.
DENT People think charities these days are too businesslike
and professional and commercial. Well I work for this
charity and that is exactly what I'm like but the charity   10
itself is full of warmth and compassion and we have all
these wonderful ladies in knitted hats.

Twenty-nine

[*The* THIEF *robs a bank.*]

Thirty

[*The* MAYOR *and* SELBY.]

MAYOR Sun. Drought. Starvation.
SELBY That's not political. It's an act of God.

Thirty-one

[DENT, SELBY *and* PRICE.]

[SELBY *is writing at a desk.* DENT *is restless.*]

DENT We'll have Price here in a minute yattering on about
his doughnuts. I hope you've learnt in your time with
me that a charity has to be run like any other business.
It exists to make money. Mr Price can talk about
Christian brotherhood and the joy of giving, and it's   5
men of vision like him who get things started. But once
you get into the day to day, what matters is the figures
at the bottom of the columns. Whether to buy the
freehold of the gift shops. Whether to leave our latest
bequest in Imperial Tobacco.° The sooner we can get   10
rid of him and get on with some real work – good
afternoon, Mr Price, nice to see you.
     [*PRICE comes in.*]
PRICE Ah Miss Selby. Hard at it as usual. You remind me
of myself at your age when I used to go out and buy a
doughnut and always put a penny –   15
DENT Miss Selby's working on some ideas for our next
publicity campaign.
PRICE Good, let's hear them.
DENT I haven't looked at them myself yet. It might save
time if you –   20
PRICE It doesn't matter if they're not good. It's the spirit in
which she does it that matters.
DENT By the time of your next visit we could select –
PRICE I want to know what goes on in everyone's head.
Are you trying to keep me out of my own charity? The   25
baker never interfered.

DENT What we're trying to do is get a hardhitting
dynamic campaign that is acceptable to the public.
Oxfam devised a commercial showing a cake with a
white hand cutting a slice and then taking the whole   30
cake and a black hand taking the slice. We want to
avoid anything like that.

PRICE It sounds rather clever.

DENT It was clever. It was accurate. It was hardhitting.
ITV wouldn't show it. They said it was political.   35

PRICE Oh well. Political. Of course we don't want to be
political. Suppose we had a cake and … oh well. Let's
listen to Miss Selby.

SELBY I thought a picture of a dead child. You can see its
ribs sticking out, its swollen stomach, clearly it starved   40
to death. Or a child that died of an illness, say measles,
it could be covered with sores, whatever you like, this
is a rough draft, you get the idea. And the caption:
'This is your fault.'

DENT No.   45

PRICE It's quite hardhitting, you know.

DENT It's out of the question. People don't like to be
blamed.

SELBY You could have a dead child, and the caption:
'Whose fault is this?'   50

DENT There can never be any suggestion of fault.

SELBY Just a picture of a dead child?

DENT No no no.

PRICE She's doing her best. It's very good for a first try,
Miss Selby. I came up with something like it once   55
myself.

DENT Look, Miss Selby, people don't like to be made
miserable. If your advertisement makes them feel bad,
they'll put it out of their minds as fast as they can. You
want something that makes them feel good. And   60
makes them feel even better when they give the money.

SELBY An advertisement about people starving that's going to make people feel good?

DENT Exactly.

PRICE It is rather a tricky one. 65

DENT Perhaps by the next time you come –

PRICE Oh I don't mind waiting. I'm enjoying myself.

DENT If you'll excuse me, I'll just be –

SELBY I've got it. I've got it. A picture of a well-fed, smiling child and the caption: 'Who makes her happy?' 70

DENT That is more like it.

PRICE I knew she could do it.

SELBY It implies, you see, that you made her happy by giving her money and you feel good and so you do go and give some money because otherwise you won't feel 75 quite so good and when you've given it you feel very good indeed.

DENT Congratulations, Miss Selby.

SELBY Well that's a relief. You had me worried there for a moment. That's my first idea okayed. Now this is my 80 second idea. It's about coffee.

DENT Oxfam tried that. People don't like –

SELBY Wait till you hear this. A cup of coffee, you see, and the caption, Does coffee cost too much? And the reader thinks yes yes, it costs me a pound a quarter, or 85 whatever it is by the time this is printed, you've got him on your side. Then you let him have it: You can afford coffee even at this high price but the people who pick it can't. What does it cost them in suffering? The extra money you pay isn't all going in wages to 90 coffee-bean pickers, don't you think it, why have coffee share prices rocketed, and tea the same – we'd have a similar one about tea – the conditions people who pick tea live in would spoil your tea party if you saw them, oh yes, and a certain tea company who shall 95 be nameless – or we might name them – made twice

the profits this year they did last year, and it all started
because Britain was a colonial power and made people
in those countries grow tea and coffee for you to drink
instead of food for themselves, and sugar too, you may   100
think sugar's gone up, my God, do you read the
business pages of your newspaper, the eyes of the
sugar world are on the talks between the EEC and the
sugar-producing countries, and the EEC doesn't want
to give them the 4 per cent increase they're asking and   105
you have the nerve to complain about immigration
when they come here looking for a better standard of
living and I hope you feel pretty sick every time you
drink a cup of tea or coffee and put sugar in it and
think where it comes from and give a whole lot of   110
money to charity because you're no better than slave
dealers and you're not drinking tea and coffee you're
drinking human blood, sweat and tears.

PRICE That's jolly good. Perhaps a little bit strong.

SELBY It doesn't have to be in exactly those words, of   115
course. We'd polish it up. I'm more than happy to
rewrite it.

DENT Wouldn't you say it was a little bit political?

PRICE Was it, Miss Selby? Oh dear. That's not what I
expected of you at all. You always seem such a nice   120
girl.

SELBY Political? Oh no no no no no. I wouldn't dream.
No. Political? Ha ha, good heavens, no no. No.

Thirty-two

[*A* WOMAN.]

WOMAN Dear sir, I have given to your charity for many
years but I will demand my money back if there are

35

any more disgusting appeals blaming me for the state
of the world. I don't mind being told a rich person has
a duty to give crumbs off his plate to the poor man at   5
the gate, but I won't stand for being told I'm wrong to
be rich, especially when I'm not. I particularly resent in
Jubilee year any suggestion that Britannia doesn't play
fair. Anyone would think from your appeal that these
people have some right to a fair share of the world's   10
resources. Next I suppose you'll be suggesting they
needn't say thank you.

Thirty-three

[DENT, SELBY *and* PRICE.]

DENT If you want to be political, Miss Selby –
SELBY No no no –
DENT If you want to suggest that there are causes of world
poverty and they are to be found largely in our systems
of trade and government, there are magazines that put   5
this point of view. We contribute to the financing of
these magazines but completely dissociate ourselves
from what they say.
SELBY Yes yes yes, I do dissociate –
PRICE I'm sure her heart is in the right place.   10
DENT In this way we help spread the idea to the few
people who may be receptive to it and get the more
subversive young people out of the charity itself, where
they're a terrible nuisance because they're the same
types who want workers' control and a place on the   15
board, when what we need is all the titles and captains
of industry we can get, so as I say we get rid of them to
these magazines and keep our own image of a

completely nonpolitical charity spreading a little
sunshine.   20

SELBY No no, I want to work for the charity. I just got
carried away by the facts. I did have this third idea, I
don't expect you want to hear it, it is hardhitting, well
we could polish it up. I thought – it's just an idea –
well what it is … is a big poster with big red letters   25
saying Fuck you, greedy pigs – no. No no no no no.
Just off the top of my head. An idea. No. Haha. No.

DENT Oxfam are selling this little book. It's a collection of
after dinner stories called *Pass the Port*. It's 'a
glittering array of famous people parting with gems of   30
wit usually reserved for their intimate friends.' It's
'what royalty, a prime minister, judges, bishops, trade
union leaders, admirals, senior academics, and
captains of industry consider to be funny in our day.'
After dinner jokes by top people. That's far more the   35
spirit.

Thirty-four

[*The* MANAGING DIRECTOR *of a tea company.*]

TEA MAN You may at this very moment be drinking a cup
of our tea. It has been alleged that my company made
twice as much profit this year as last year. In fact we
made twice as much profit this year as last year. But
really you know the conditions of our tea pickers   5
aren't so abysmally frightful as when people first
started criticising us. We've improved their conditions
so they are now only as frightful as those of people
doing similar work in these countries. It would be
ridiculous to expect us to raise their wages to anything   10
approaching yours, although of course we'd love to do

that, because they would then be far better off than
their neighbours. I hope you'll feel better about our tea
when you think that not just the tea pickers but
everyone in those countries is living in what you would   15
consider for your own family to be appalling
destitution – everyone of that class, I should say,
because there are of course people in every country of
the free world who are enormously rich, just as there
are in this country.   20

Thirty-five

[*The* THIEF *running along the roof of a train.*]

Thirty-six

[DENT.]

DENT I have been under attack for the way I run our gift
shops. These shops sell goods made in poor – sorry,
underdeveloped, sorry, developing – countries,
providing a livelihood for the craftsmen, cheap gifts
for you and a profit for us to put back into the charity.   5
It has been suggested we are taking too much profit
but we are paying the workers a more than fair wage
in terms of their own country. It's because labour is so
cheap there that we are able to sell the goods cheap to
you and if they weren't cheap you wouldn't buy them.   10
A charity is a business and the profits are put to good
use and we can't raise their living standards to
anything approaching yours because – and anyway
we're only talking about a tiny fraction of the
population, do you think charities deal in large sums   15

38

of money, England spends as much on defence in a
year as all the rich countries together spend on aid,
and aid is massive compared to charity, what are we
talking about? We sell hanging baskets made of jute
from Bangladesh. Britain has frozen jute out of our   20
markets. What's a few thousand hanging baskets? So
there's no need at all to get at me for the way I run our
gift shops.

Thirty-seven

[*The* MAYOR *and* SELBY.]

MAYOR Sun?
SELBY Sun.
MAYOR Sun, moon, planets, space programme, cost of.
SELBY That's American politics.
MAYOR Sun, heat, alternative source of energy, you see   5
    where we're getting, dangers of nuclear power,
    Windscale° fast breeder, future of coal industry – Or
    again, sun, Spain, holidays, rate of exchange –
SELBY All right, all right.
MAYOR My snakes aren't political at all.   10

Thirty-eight

[*The* THIEF *kidnaps* SIR ARTHUR *at gunpoint into a car.*]

Thirty-nine

[SELBY, PRICE *and* DENT.]

SELBY Nobody sells cigarettes. Or margarine. Or
  breakfast cereal. They sell getting more girls or
  pleasing your man or being a good mum. We're too
  direct, selling poor countries. We must sell what
  people want. All right, they want to feel good about   5
  the starving millions, but there's plenty of things they
  want more than that.
PRICE But charity is more spiritual than margarine.
DENT Charity is business. You're a businessman, Mr Price.
PRICE Yes, I've tried to run my business with an eye to   10
  charity.
DENT And your charity with an eye to business. Charity is
  inseparable from capitalism.

Forty

[*A* MOTHER *and her* BABY.]

[*The* MOTHER *is holding the* BABY, *who puts a coin in a
collecting-box.*]

VOICE Build a safe world – for him.

Forty-one

[*A* MAN *and a* GIRL.]

[*The* MAN *puts a necklace round the* GIRL'*s neck, then writes a cheque while she leans over admiringly.*]

VOICE When you want to give her the world, give to her favourite charity.

Forty-two

[COWBOYS; *a* CHILD.]

[*The* COWBOYS *shoot it out.*]

[*A lone survivor walks out. He sees a* CHILD *with a begging bowl. He tosses money into it.*]

VOICE A man's gotta do what a man's gotta do – give.

Forty-three

[*The* THIEF, SIR ARTHUR *and* SELBY.]

[*The* THIEF *and* SIR ARTHUR *are in a bare room.*]

[*The* THIEF *and* SELBY *talk through the locked door.*]

SELBY I'm not armed.

THIEF Twenty thousand, five hundred and ninety-six
pounds I've got for you already. That's the train
robbery, the bank robbery and various odds and ends.
And when they pay the ransom you'll have another   5
half million.

SELBY That's very kind of you.

THIEF Think what it's going to buy. Wells. Tractors. Eye
operations.

SELBY But we can't accept money got by crime.   10

THIEF Crime? Whose crime? Isn't it their crime having it
when people are starving?

SELBY Yes but –

THIEF You don't deny that Robin Hood is a folk hero?

SELBY No but –   15

THIEF Then whose side are you on?

SELBY But people have to give the money themselves
because they want to or it's not charity.

THIEF Look, the reason I went into this. I've got friends
who do the same thing but in their case for political   20
motives. They rob banks for liberation movements.
But I'm a pacifist. I don't want the money I steal spent
on guns. I'd rather have it spent on medicines. I'd
rather give it to poor farmers to buy equipment. I'm

aiming to personally redistribute the wealth of the   25
world.

SELBY Singlehanded?

THIEF If I devote my whole life to it. And other people will
follow my example. Are you trying to put me down for
only having half a million pounds? It's going to add up.   30

SELBY There's quite a lot of money to be shifted.

THIEF You tell me who's ever given half a million to your
charity. If everyone who gives 50p now raised half a
million we'd be getting somewhere. I reckon in about
fifty years the world will be transformed.   35

SELBY But what about all the governments and … You
can't transform the world just by getting money from
individuals.

THIEF Then what are you in a charity for? You sound like
my friends in liberation. But I don't agree. I believe in   40
charities. If every man, woman and child in the
western world stole a thousand pounds a year –

SELBY I think you should consider letting Sir Arthur go.

THIEF Unilever° invests as much in Africa in a couple of
days as you raise in a whole year. You're like kids   45
spending pocket money. So what are you going to do
about it?

SELBY We accept that we can do very little.

THIEF You do?

SELBY Yes.   50

THIEF You help a few hundred people out of millions and
you accept that?

SELBY What else can we do if that's all people give?

THIEF You take it from them.

SELBY Not by stealing it.   55

THIEF How else? I'm not interested in politics. I believe in
charities. If his company doesn't pay the ransom by
midnight I'm going to shoot him. And if your charity
doesn't accept the money I'm going to shoot him. And

if you stand out there saying stupid things I'm going to 60
shoot you. So think about it.

Forty-four

[*The* MAYOR.]

MAYOR A favourite pet of mine is the rubber boa, a small
snake perhaps twenty inches long, whose tail looks
very much like its head. When it meets an enemy it
curls up in a ball and sticks out its tail and waves it
about so it looks like the head of a striking snake. If 5
the enemy attacks the tail, the rubber boa brings out
its head and bites it. They're not normally aggressive
though so they make a good pet, the only trouble is,
being a burrowing snake, he's usually under the earth
in his pen and I don't see as much of him as I would 10
like.

Forty-five

[DENT, SELBY *and* PRICE.]

DENT It's most important not to come to the end of the
financial year with too large a balance or people will
think we don't know what to do with the money.
SELBY What are we going to do with the money?
DENT That's what we don't know. 5
PRICE I never remember why that's a problem. Can't we
just send Miss Selby with a big bag of notes and she
could walk about handing them to the poor people. I'd
go myself if I was younger. Oh I'd love to do that and
see their happy faces. 10

DENT It's a bit more complicated than that.

PRICE Yes, to be fair we should share it out equally. Just to give me an idea, what would one million pounds come to divided among the most destitute people in the world, not including everyone worse off than us, 15 but the ones we can really hardly bear to imagine, just as a rough estimate for planning purposes?

DENT Roughly one thousandth of a penny each.

PRICE Well. I'll have to resign myself yet again to not being able to help everyone. But even one life saved, 20 one person made happy, has its value. Perhaps we should make it simple and Miss Selby should go out to India or Africa or South America and the first person she meets give him the whole million. That would at least make one very happy Indian. 25

DENT When I say we don't know what to do with the money I don't mean we don't know what to do with the money.

SELBY Of course not.

DENT We have plenty of agents and field-workers looking 30 for the best possible projects. But what with the sheikh and the commercials and Sir Arthur's legacy we have a greater surplus than usual and I'd like to find some really special use for it.

PRICE The sheikh has just built a large hospital in the 35 desert. Why don't we send Miss Selby out to get some ideas?

Forty-six

[*An* AMERICAN PATIENT, SELBY *and an* ARAB GARDENER.]

[*The* PATIENT *is in a wheelchair in a flowery garden.*]

[*The* GARDENER *stands hosing the lawn.*]

PATIENT When I had a heart attack I thought the end had come. I was frightened even to cut my finger in this country. There's people dying of disease everywhere, no sanitation, no doctors, nothing. But we radioed for help and a helicopter brought me two hundred miles to 5 the hospital. And it's just great. I've got a private room, pretty nurses, vases of flowers from this wonderful garden. If I wanted a heart transplant they could do it, that's how good this hospital is.

SELBY I suppose people come here from all over the place? 10

PATIENT There's a woman flew a thousand miles to have her nose shortened. It has real international prestige.

SELBY And anyone who's ill in any of the villages in the country, they come here?

PATIENT If they can get here, sure. If you've no transport 15 and you're feeling sick, I guess not too many of them bother.

SELBY You mean most of the people are getting no medical treatment at all?

PATIENT I guess not. But you have to set that against the 20 fact that the treatment provided here is of the very highest quality. Just as this garden blooms in the desert on account of they have hoses playing on the lawn day and night.

SELBY And outside the gate it's clouds of dust blowing   25
about.

PATIENT That's right. Isn't it great?

SELBY It's not so great if you live outside the gate.

PATIENT Yes, it's a very unfortunate thing there's no piped
water in the villages. I've got some wonderful   30
photographs of the women carrying big jars on their
heads. I guess you'd say the men should carry it on
their heads too. But some of the men get to work in
the garden.

SELBY For the money they've spent on this hospital they   35
could have some sort of medical worker in every
village.

PATIENT Sure, and what's a medical worker? I wouldn't
want some highschool kid looking after me, and why
should they? This hospital has some of the richest   40
patients in the world, and they want the best just like
we do in the west. You can't have heart transplants in
every village. I can tell you I wouldn't be alive today if
it wasn't for this hospital.

SELBY Yes but hundreds of people die in this country who   45
never –

PATIENT Are you saying it doesn't matter whether or not I
am alive today?

SELBY No but –

PATIENT What's the matter with you anyway? This   50
hospital cures sick people and makes a damn good job
of it. OK?

Forty-seven

[DENT *and* SELBY.]

[*They are talking to each other on the phone.*]

DENT It doesn't make sense to give money to a country
that's far richer than Britain even if the people are
poorer. Well we do, I can think of examples, but not
an oil state, really.

SELBY Then we must make the sheikh share out the   5
money to the benefit of the people. Is there no one
trying to do that already? There must surely be groups
of people in the country who want the wealth to be in
the hands of – sorry.

DENT They're called guerrillas.   10

SELBY Sorry.

DENT In Oman* the British Army is fighting –

SELBY Look I'm not trying to be political, I'm trying to be
sensible. I don't know why I keep –

DENT All right, we'll say no more about it. Go to a   15
different country. Go somewhere unquestionably poor.
Go to Bangladesh. Even with all the aid that's been
poured in it's still full of hungry people.
Straightforward need.

Forty-eight

[*A* VILLAIN *and a* PEASANT.]

[*A silent movie of* A Year in Bangladesh: *mime, captions, music. The* VILLAIN *has the top hat and moustache of melodrama. The* PEASANT *is in rags.*]

1 **The Landlord**
[*The VILLAIN demands the rent. The PEASANT gives him sacks.*]
[*Caption: 'Here's the rent, sir, half my grain.'*]

2 **The Moneylender**
[*The same VILLAIN, this time as a moneylender sitting at a table with bags of money. The PEASANT is pleading with him.*]   5
[*Captions: 'We've eaten our half of the grain. Can you lend me some money until the harvest?'*]
[*'Certainly. The interest is 200%.'*]

3 **The Merchant at Harvest Time**
[*The same VILLAIN, this time as a merchant. The*   10
PEASANT with sacks.]
[*Captions: 'It's been a good harvest. If I sell nearly all my crop I can pay my debt.'*]
[*'Everyone's selling. The price is very low.'*]

4 **The Merchant Six Months Later**
[*The VILLAIN as before. The PEASANT with a little*   15
money.]
[*Captions: 'I've no food left for my family. I want to buy some.'*]
[*'Everyone's buying. The price has doubled.'*]

5 **The Landlord Again**
[*The distraught PEASANT on his knees before the*   20
VILLAIN.]
[*Caption: 'If you can't pay the rent you'll be evicted.'*]

6 **The Charity**
[*The PEASANT with a begging bowl.*]

Forty-nine

[SELBY, *on the phone.*]

SELBY You know I recommended we buy boats for the
fishermen ... Well, there is a bit of bother, yes ... I am
getting on with it, I'm getting round to it. You know
the fishermen used to rent boats from these rich
boat-owners who charged them so much and ... Last   5
night the boat-owners smashed up the boats. Not their
boats, the fishermen's boats. Our boats ... Rented the
boat-owners' boats of course and gone fishing ... Yes,
that's what I'm doing, finding another project, yes.

Fifty

[*The* LADY *in the knitted hat.*]

LADY A message from the publicity department. We have
a wonderful charity gift shop in Johannesburg which is
great fun and highly successful. The variety of things
sold is almost as astounding as the variety of
customers, some of them hard-pressed blacks looking   5
for cheap clothes, others arriving in Jags in the hope of
finding antiques.

Fifty-one

[*A* MINISTER.]

MINISTER I have just come from the North–South
conference between the rich and poor countries. And
I've come to reassure you that we are not going to give
them anything like what they are asking for. We are
not going to wipe out their debts nor finance a   5
common fund to stabilise their export prices. On the
other hand, we are going to cancel some of their debts
and give a little support to some kind of fund, because
if we let these countries get too poor they won't be
able to buy our goods, with disastrous effects on our   10
own economy. Also the oil-producing countries are
eager for us to help their less fortunate brothers. If we
don't they might not sell us oil at a price we can afford
to pay. Nobody likes to see millions of people living in
misery, and I won't lose any votes if I tell you we are   15
going to help them just enough to help ourselves.

Fifty-two

[*The* LADY *in the knitted hat.*]

LADY A message from the publicity department.
   [*A still of two old black women; her voice over.*]
These poor old ladies live not only on a rubbish dump
but in a very violent area. When our photographer
took this picture he narrowly escaped having his
camera smashed by young troublemakers throwing   5

stones. But the old ladies somehow survive without being attacked.

Fifty-three

[*A film of a hurricane.*]

Fifty-four

[DENT *and* PRICE.]

DENT I thought we were never going to get the money spent. Miss Selby seems to be incapable of recommending a project. But now, thank God, we can transfer it to the hurricane disaster fund.

PRICE Yes, God seems to have solved the problem for us.   5 We'll send Miss Selby straight to the scene of the disaster.

Fifty-five

[SELBY *and another* PASSENGER *on a plane.*]

PASSENGER You worried by takeoff?

SELBY Not very.

PASSENGER Landing's worse.

SELBY Yes.

PASSENGER Especially if there's no landing strip.   5

SELBY No landing strip?

PASSENGER I imagine it's been blown away. Or buried under ten feet of mud. Or scattered all over with uprooted trees.

SELBY The control tower would tell the pilot. 10

PASSENGER You think so?

SELBY You think not?

PASSENGER Well it doesn't bother me, because the hazards
of takeoff and landing are nothing to the journey itself.
It's just starting to get dangerous now. 15

SELBY It says we can undo our seat-belts.

PASSENGER Hi-jackers.

SELBY What? Where?

PASSENGER I carry a cyanide capsule.

SELBY What? Why? 20

PASSENGER You see people get up. You think they're just
going to the bathroom. But suddenly one of them pulls
a gun.

SELBY Not on every flight.

PASSENGER I'll be ready. I'll kill myself rather than fall into 25
their hands. I'm telling you so you won't get a shock
when I keel over. There now, watch that one.

SELBY But it could be anyone. It could be me.

PASSENGER Well I'm telling you, you won't pull a fast one
on me because I have my cyanide capsule. 30

SELBY It isn't me.

PASSENGER It could be you.

SELBY It couldn't be me because I work for a charity
organisation and we don't get involved in any kind of
political activity and that includes hi-jacking planes. 35

PASSENGER You going to give out blankets and all that
stuff?

SELBY I'm hoping to be the very first charity worker on
the scene.

PASSENGER Do you know the greatest tragedy of this 40
hurricane?

SELBY Tell me and I'll see what I can do.

PASSENGER Bananas.

SELBY Bananas?

PASSENGER Do you know how much you guys at home are   45
  going to have to pay for bananas next winter?

SELBY How much?

PASSENGER And do you know whose fault that is?

SELBY The hurricane?

PASSENGER The peasants. The people you are coming to   50
  wrap up in blankets.

SELBY I'm sure they didn't mean to.

PASSENGER They chopped down the trees. They chopped
  down the trees on the hillside. So when the wind and
  rain came pouring down there was nothing to hold the   55
  earth on the hills and smash glub yuk, there's mud ten
  feet deep over all the bananas in the valley.

SELBY Well I never did like bananas all that much.

PASSENGER Wait, watch that one.

SELBY Why, what did he do? What? What?   60

PASSENGER He acted normal.

SELBY What did they cut the trees down for?

PASSENGER Because they're stupid, I guess. To grow food.
  The landowners who arranged for us to have the valley
  to grow bananas should have spelt it out to the people: 65
  if you cut down the trees, there's going to be soil
  erosion. But nobody told them. They cut down the
  trees. Wallop.

SELBY It walloped them too. There's 8,000 dead.

PASSENGER Yes, that's right, they brought all these tons of   70
  rocks and mud down on their heads. If they want to
  kill themselves, OK, but they don't have to wreck the
  bananas.

SELBY Where did they used to grow food then? Before
  they went up the hills and cut down the trees?   75

PASSENGER Are you trying to get funny?

SELBY No, I just wondered where –

PASSENGER You know perfectly well where they used to
  live.

SELBY No I don't. 80

PASSENGER In the valleys of course, where we grow the bananas. Do you have any idea of the importance of the export of bananas to the business community of this country and to my company?

SELBY No. Yes. 85

PASSENGER Then you've some idea of the immensity of this tragedy. I won't go into the figures. It puts a strain on my heart. I'll just close my eyes and meditate for twenty minutes.

SELBY Excuse me. Excuse me. Oh please, excuse me. 90

PASSENGER It's not good for me to be interrupted when I'm meditating.

SELBY I just wanted to get one thing clear.

PASSENGER It makes me very irritable if I'm disturbed just when I'm getting calm. 95

SELBY Are you saying the 8,000 deaths in this hurricane were caused by the landowners and the banana companies taking the valleys to grow bananas?

PASSENGER Are you some kind of a communist? Are you going to hi-jack this airplane? 100

SELBY No.

PASSENGER Why don't you hi-jack this airplane and go to Cuba?

SELBY Why don't you take your cyanide capsule?

PASSENGER Stewardess! 105

SELBY No, really, I just –

PASSENGER Stewardess, I've caught a hi-jacker.

SELBY No, really, there's been a misunderstanding.

Fifty-six

[SELBY. *She is backed up against bales of blankets she is handing out with one hand while trying to take photographs with the other.*]

SELBY Look I'm trying to take some photographs for our
  publicity, do you mind? Give the blanket back and I'll
  give it to you again, and this time I want you to smile,
  right? Smile? Smile? Does anyone here speak English?
  Cheese, cheese, formaggio. No, it's all right, you can   5
  have the blanket back, I just want –

Fifty-seven

[SELBY *and a* GIRL. *Both are dirty and exhausted.*]

SELBY Was that three nights without sleep?
GIRL I've lost count.
SELBY Well, I've finished. Every last bit of sticking plaster.
GIRL Yes, I've finished too.
SELBY Well.   5
GIRL Yeh.
SELBY And tomorrow start planning the long-term relief.
GIRL Don't talk about it.
SELBY At least there's no problem seeing what has to be
  done.   10
GIRL What has to be done?
SELBY Build the houses again. Put everything back like it
  was before.
GIRL You're planning to build another slum are you?
SELBY Let's think about it tomorrow.   15

GIRL Why do you think there's 8,000 dead?

SELBY The hurricane … and well the erosion, of course, the mud, the banana companies can't be left out of it. On the other hand they were very flimsy huts. Proper houses. 20

GIRL So there's 8,000 dead because of what it was like before?

SELBY Yes.

GIRL So you're going to spend your charity's share of the disaster relief fund putting everything back like it was 25 before.

SELBY I thought you were tired.

GIRL I am.

SELBY Look, be realistic. Ninety per cent of the people here own 10 per cent of the land, right? You told me 30 so yourself. And 3 per cent of the people own all the best land and grow bananas and sugar for export. Therefore, it's perfectly obvious that anything we can do with the relief money is bound to be leaving everything like it was before unless the whole society 35 changes. All we can do is patch things up.

GIRL Some of the peasants have formed a league. The landowners don't like it. Two men were shot when they went to a union meeting.

SELBY Yes I know, it's very sad, but 8,000 – 40

GIRL There's talk of occupying some uncultivated land and the peasants' league growing food collectively.

SELBY There's always unrest after a disaster.

GIRL I'm going to recommend to my lot we use our share of the disaster fund to support the peasants' league. 45

SELBY I thought a hurricane would be … you know … earthquakes, floods. Natural disasters.

GIRL A hurricane is just a strong wind. An earthquake is just the earth moving. They're not disasters till you get people. 50

57

SELBY I thought ... you know ... you can't blame anyone. Act of God.

Fifty-eight

[*The* MAYOR *and* SELBY.]

MAYOR Act of God. Earthquake. Guatemala. Shockproof houses, wealthy inhabitants, mostly all right. Shacks on ravines, in Guatemala City alone 1,200 dead, 90,000 homeless. In the whole country, 22,000 dead, mostly the poor –   5

SELBY All right.

MAYOR City official shot dead after suggesting homeless people should rebuild on unoccupied private land.

SELBY All right.

MAYOR Name a nonpolitical natural disaster.   10

SELBY Drought. Drought in the Sahel.

MAYOR Really?

SELBY Go on.

MAYOR Sahel. French colonial rule. Change in people's way of life. Cattle routes blocked, traditional rights to   15 wells disregarded, crops they couldn't eat, overgrazing of pasture, people concentrated round a few wells instead of –

SELBY I get the idea.

MAYOR Act of God. No rain. Drought. Traditional ways   20 of surviving drought gone. No reserves of food. Too many cattle for the pasture. Too many people in one area.

SELBY I said I get the idea.

MAYOR Famine.   25

SELBY Yes.

MAYOR All right?
SELBY An act of God is political, all right.

Fifty-nine

[SELBY, *a* GUERRILLA *and a* JOURNALIST.]

[SELBY *is sitting under a tree.*]

[*The* GUERRILLA *stands nearby with a gun.*]

[*The* JOURNALIST *approaches cautiously.*]

SELBY Are you really there?
JOURNALIST Yes.
SELBY Because sometimes I see things.
JOURNALIST No, I'm a journalist.
SELBY Am I being rescued?   5
JOURNALIST I'm being allowed a five-minute interview.
SELBY Take this message.
JOURNALIST It's three months since you disappeared after
    sending a message back to your office that you wanted
    to learn more about the country before returning to   10
    London. It's been established that you then set off in a
    jeep. How soon were you captured by guerrillas?
SELBY The first day.
JOURNALIST And could you tell me how that capture took
    place?   15
SELBY To Mr Dent, the director. And Mr Price.
JOURNALIST And how are you being treated?
SELBY This is the message. Our share of the disaster
    emergency fund should be divided between the
    peasants' league and the liberation movement.   20

JOURNALIST The guerrillas are demanding a ransom. That is the condition for your release? How much –

SELBY Their aim is to overthrow the government and introduce land reform.

JOURNALIST How much are they demanding?   25

SELBY So tell Mr Price, the best way to help the people here is to help them with what they're doing, which is organise to fight oppression, and the quarter of a million pounds should all be given to help that struggle.

JOURNALIST They are demanding a quarter of a million   30
pounds ransom and have submitted you to a gruelling session of brainwashing.

SELBY Tell them I'm getting a bit bored sitting here under the tree. It gets very hot.

JOURNALIST And how exactly were you captured?   35

Sixty

[PRICE *and some* BUSINESSMEN.]

[PRICE *is presiding over a businessmen's lunch. There are bananas on every plate.*]

PRICE We've all made so much money importing bananas that I'm sure we'll be glad to give a little of it to charity, especially when we can have fun at the same time.

Sixty-one

[PRICE, DENT, SELBY, GUERRILLAS, PEASANTS *and*
BUSINESSMEN.]

[*A sideshow. The* GUERRILLAS *and the* PEASANTS *stand at
the back of a rifle-range being shot at by* BUSINESSMEN. *As
they are wounded they crawl off and are replaced by others.
Behind the stall,* PRICE, DENT *and* SELBY *are bandaging
wounds and sending them back in.*]

SELBY I'll have you patched up in no time and then you
can go and be shot at again.

Sixty-two

[*The* MAYOR.]

MAYOR The royal python is another lovely snake, known
also as the ball python, no doubt from its habit of
curling up into a tight ball when alarmed. You can roll
it along the table just like a real ball. But you can't
force it to unwind, the more you force it the more
frightened it gets and the tighter it stays rolled up.
They like to eat live food, of course, but you can feed
them in captivity on raw beef if you cover it with
chicken feathers or rabbit fur.

5

Sixty-three

[PRICE *and* SELBY.]

[SELBY *is in a hospital bed.* PRICE *is visiting.*]

PRICE It's lucky those soldiers rescued you when they did because we'd already allocated the quarter of a million, you know, for rebuilding houses and for an old people's home and an orphanage for a hundred children, so that we couldn't have paid the ransom if 5 we'd wanted to. And you weren't even caught in the crossfire.

SELBY I was very lucky.

PRICE And you're feeling better, are you? Because when you first arrived back in England you were quite 10 delirious. I'm sure you've forgotten the things you said to me. And I've decided to forget them too.

SELBY I'm fine now, thank you.

PRICE You must have as long a holiday as you need, and let me know when you feel up to working again. 15

SELBY If it's all right with you, Mr Price, I think I'd like a break from the charity side of things.

PRICE It's what I like to see, Miss Selby, a young person spending a year or two working for charity and then coming back into the business. You've gained a great 20 deal of experience and bring more to your work. You've certainly done your bit and it's high time you got on with your career. I'll be able to bring you in at management level.

Sixty-four

[SELBY *sitting behind a large desk.*]

Sixty-five

[SELBY *and the* MAYOR.]

SELBY Snake. Snakeskin. Handbags. Rich –
MAYOR Yes.
SELBY You must have seen that all along.
MAYOR Everyone has his little blind spot. I love my snakes.
Relatively speaking, I would still go so far as to say a   5
snake is not essentially political. A live snake is hardly
political at all compared to anything you like to name.
Name something.

Sixty-six

[SELBY *sitting behind a large desk.*]

Three More
Sleepless Nights

♦

Notes on layout

A speech usually follows the one immediately before it BUT:

1) When one character starts speaking before the other has finished, the point of interruption is marked /, e.g.:

MARGARET I don't dislike him / but that don't mean I
    fancy him.
FRANK And he don't dislike you. Eh? Has he said that?
    He don't dislike you? He don't dislike you.

2) A character sometimes continues speaking right through another's speech, e.g.:

MARGARET Your friend. I don't like him /
FRANK You fancy him.
MARGARET like that, I quite like him.

This applies even when the intervening speech is very long.

Characters

Margaret

Frank

Pete

Dawn

There are three scenes which happen in different rooms but the set is the same all through, a double bed.

Three More Sleepless Nights was first staged at the Soho Poly, London on 9 June 1980. The cast was as follows:

Margaret,   Jan Chappell

Frank,   Fred Pearson

Pete,   Kevin McNally

Dawn,   Harriet Walter

Directed by Les Waters

One

MARGARET Night after night you're round there, don't
bother lying, night after night, you can clear out round
and live there, I don't care. Night after night / coming
home pissed, what am I for,

FRANK Shut it. 5

MARGARET clean up your mess? Times I've cleaned your
sick off the floor, you was sick on the Christmas
presents Christmas Eve, time you shat yourself / tell
her that, she'd like that, clean up your shit.

FRANK Shut it. 10

MARGARET Give her something to think about. She thinks
the sun shines out of your arse, I could tell her
different, ten years / of you, let her try ten

FRANK Shut up will you, five minutes peace, come through
my own front door you start rucking. What sort of 15
home's that? Any wonder I don't come home, when I
come in you start, any wonder, Christ.

MARGARET years, she don't know half, spruce yourself up
aftershave me mum give you Christmas, she don't
know who you are, thinks you walked out the telly, 20
that's what you fancy, someone don't know nothing
about you. You can come over big, talk big, big
spender, Mr Big, Mr Big Pig coming home night after
night / pissed out of your mind, what mind you got to
be pissed out of? 25

FRANK Shut up will you. I've not been there. I've not been
to see her two weeks now, not been round there two
weeks, I told you I was stopping seeing her. She come
up the garage dinner-time. I says no, I told Margaret
I'm not seeing you and it's true I'm not seeing her, ask 30

anyone, ask Charlie. I been up the pub that's all. / I
suppose I'm not let go up the pub now is

MARGARET Ask Charlie.

FRANK it, sorry mates my wife won't let me. I been up the
pub, I been to Charlie's for a few pints after, ask   35
Charlie / ask anyone, my wife's just checking

MARGARET Charlie'd say anything.

FRANK up on me, she don't believe a word I say, don't
believe a word I say, don't believe a word I say, do
you? / What sort of marriage, what sort of   40

MARGARET Ask her, shall I?

FRANK wife are you? What sort of marriage? What's left?
What do I bother for? What I give her up for?

MARGARET Go round there shall I, ask her, silly cow, she'd
tell me too, all smiles, tears in her eyes, can't we be   45
friends, can we fuck, must have been desperate to be
friends with her anyone with a pram and a cup of tea, /
can't think what

FRANK Might as well still see her, might as well go round
there now. Your fault, you drive me, you drive me   50
round there, don't believe a word, what's the point,
you think I'm having it off, come in the door start
rucking, might as well enjoy it.

MARGARET you see in her, her hair's growing out too, looks
dreadful, looks cheap, she's cheap, word my mum was   55
fond of, cheap, see the point of it now, cheap. She
don't look younger than me, she's five years, what you
must think of me if you fancy that. Try to look after
myself, / don't

FRANK I go round there now you know whose fault it is,   60
what sort of marriage is this? What sort of wife are
you? Come in my own front door.

MARGARET look bad, could have been a model, could have
been a hairdresser, could have been a shorthand typist
easy the grades I had in Commerce, I had good speeds,   65

could have been a temp made a fortune by now,
secretary to an executive / gave it up to be a wife to
you, could have took the pill

FRANK Yeah yeah yeah yeah yeah.

MARGARET gone raving, could have had blokes wouldn't   70
look at her, cheap she is, hair growing out, stupid cow,
can't type even, can't read, what you must think of me
if you fancy that. Puts you in your place, what you
must be like, must be desperate, feeling your age a bit,
take what's on offer, last chance, think what other   75
blokes she's had / can't hold jobs, weirdos, that's
where

FRANK You fancy Charlie.

MARGARET you're heading. Weirdos and winos, about it
with her, all she can get. There was one looked like a   80
goldfish couldn't shut his mouth come in handy I
suppose with the kissing, surprised you can shut yours
/ all the time you spend round

FRANK You fancy Charlie.

MARGARET there, want to watch out you don't end up   85
looking like a goldfish. I do not fancy Charlie /

FRANK You like him don't you?

MARGARET so don't start that. I quite like him. He's your
friend. You're the one he tells

FRANK We all know whose friend he is, you like him don't   90
you?

MARGARET lies for. Your friend. I don't like him / like

FRANK You fancy him.

MARGARET that, I quite like him.

FRANK You quite like him, you quite like what you get,   95
you quite like it, / you like it.

MARGARET I don't get nothing.

FRANK You don't get nothing. Not for want of trying. /

MARGARET I don't try. I don't know what you're talking
about   100

FRANK Not for want of trying is it. No you don't try, too good aren't you, fancy yourself, he's not pulled that easy, you've no style, no class / he's got them queuing up, Charlie.

MARGARET I don't want Charlie, I'm not interested, I love you. 105

FRANK And you like him.

MARGARET I don't dislike him / but that don't mean I fancy him.

FRANK And he don't dislike you. Eh? Has he said that? He don't dislike you? He don't / dislike you. 110

MARGARET He's not said nothing.

FRANK That's a lie, never stops talking to you, / every

MARGARET He's not said he dislikes me.

FRANK time I take you up the pub. I'm sure he hasn't said he dislikes you / no, he wouldn't. 115

MARGARET He hasn't said he likes me either.

FRANK Hasn't said he likes you? My heart bleeds. I'm very sorry he hasn't said he likes you. You'll have to make do with him touching you up. / 120

MARGARET He don't.

FRANK You're wasting your time, seems to me. Don't know why you don't get on with it / instead of

MARGARET Nothing to get on with.

FRANK making me hang about. Nothing to get on with? He thinks there is / oh yes he does. 125

MARGARET How do you know what he thinks?

FRANK Oh it's only you knows what he thinks is it? / What does he think? I should ask him, phone

MARGARET I don't know what he thinks. 130

FRANK him up, ask him / go on, phone him

MARGARET Don't be stupid.

FRANK up, ask him. He might say no he don't fancy you, that would hurt your feelings / that would

MARGARET No it wouldn't. 135

FRANK be a shock. Charlie not fancy you. I don't see why
not, it would hurt my feelings if it was me, you ent got
no feelings that's your trouble, think you're wonderful,
don't care what nobody thinks of you. Just as well /
way your skin's going   140

MARGARET He's just a friend. He's your friend.

FRANK nobody's going to want to know. You're putting
on weight too. You be friendly, I'm not bothered, you
be friendly, you take him to the pictures, don't you
stop for me. I'm not bothered. I'd move out if I was   145
you, go on / why don't you move out leave me in
peace, come in

MARGARET I don't want to move out, I love you, why don't
you listen to me, what you doing to us, what's it for?

FRANK my own front door start rucking. You want it both   150
ways don't you, me and him, well I'm not playing that
little game. Like him do you, I like him, bet he's got a
big one eh? gets big for you eh? you'd like that
wouldn't you? get all wet thinking of him eh? / think
of him in bed   155

MARGARET Night after night you come home pissed, I've
had enough of you, serve you right if I did fancy
Charlie, what if I did, what about you and her, round
there every night, I know you are whatever you say.

FRANK do you? lying there thinking of him then give me a   160
rucking, thinking of him were you? think of him when
you're with me? pretend it's him do you? eh? Wasting
your time there because Charlie wouldn't touch you if
you was the last woman, he's said that to me, he's said
that, only that time he was drunk last Christmas, you   165
couldn't keep your hands off him at the party, I was
ashamed to know where to look in front of my friends
/ if Charlie wasn't my mate

MARGARET Where were you then, upstairs with her, that's
where you were, Christmas party, who was sick on the   170
presents?

FRANK I'd break his neck, he knows that, he apologised to
me, he didn't know what he was doing could have
been his grandmother under the mistletoe if she come
at him the way you did. I didn't know where to look,   175
showing me up in front of my friends, at least what I
do I do decent, I don't shame nobody, I take her
different places than what I take you / don't go the
same pub,

MARGARET Take her with a different prick do you?   180

FRANK nothing, nobody knows, I don't flirt like you do,
it's all right between me and her, it's not flirting, it's
something special you wouldn't understand, /

MARGARET All right is it?

FRANK I go in her door don't get this / don't get   185

MARGARET I don't understand, I don't want to understand.

FRANK rucking, get some peace after a day's work, talk
about cheap, you're cheap / anyone

MARGARET Piss off round there then and I hope it's
something special and I hope you get a hot dinner with   190
it and your socks washed –

CHILD [*off*] Mummy.

FRANK you can rub up against at a party, nobody's
interested are they that's the trouble, you don't want
me, that's what it is, you don't want me, you'd have   195
anyone else you could get, you don't want me, you
can't get nobody else /

CHILD [*off*] Mummy.

FRANK that's all it is / You don't want me.

MARGARET Shut up, shush, wait.   200

    [*Silence*]

FRANK Go on then go and see him, don't mind me,
everyone's more important than me / just has to

MARGARET He'll go off, sh.

FRANK call out, drop everything.

    [*Silence*]

MARGARET I don't want a row. / Put out the light.   205

FRANK I don't want a row. I want a good night's sleep
    before tomorrow. Set the clock have you? /

MARGARET 'Course I've set the clock.

FRANK Didn't go off this morning.

MARGARET That was yesterday. It went off all right this   210
    morning / you didn't wake up, that's all.

FRANK Whichever day it was. Set it properly have you?
    [*FRANK puts out the light*]
    You don't enjoy it with me, you don't want me that's
    what it is, you don't / enjoy it with me, you

MARGARET Oh God.   215

FRANK said that I remember every word you say, you said
    that, don't deny it, you said it, / can't

MARGARET I said it once, I said I didn't enjoy it that time, I
    didn't say I don't enjoy it.

FRANK get out of it now. No man wants a woman don't   220
    want him, stands to reason, only human, Christ, you
    think I'm a fucking machine, you got a washing
    machine, drying machine, fucking machine / I'm not
    your fucking fucking machine.

MARGARET Didn't enjoy it that time my God you was   225
    drunk, you just been with her, you said she was better
    than me, she moved about more, what am I supposed
    to do? I'd had a day and a half with the kids, Johnny
    had tonsillitis / you never come

FRANK You're talking about a year ago.   230

MARGARET home till late, you said you'd be in, I'd cooked
    spaghetti and you never come home, Johnny wouldn't
    stay in bed till I hit him, not move about, I'm surprised
    I was conscious, move about more, hell, what does she

do, do it in a track suit does she? / go jogging, do it   235
while she's jogging?

FRANK Look, I don't think she's better than you, why am I
still with you? I think you're the greatest, that's why I
stopped seeing her, you're better than she is / I
stopped, I give her up, you don't believe me what's the   240
point, I might as well go and see her again, I'll go
tomorrow night, don't expect me home because I
won't be home tomorrow night.

MARGARET I'm not going in for this competition, I don't
care who's winning your little prize because I'm not   245
going in for it. I don't have to compete because I'm
your wife, you're already mine, I won already, some
prize / I'm not competing. Why

    [*FRANK puts the light on*]

FRANK Is there anything to drink?

MARGARET should I have to pull my stomach in for you, is   250
my hair all right, you're who I live with, I'm not going
in for it, I'm not putting make-up on in bed. / If she's
what you want, if that's

FRANK I've had a hard day.

MARGARET the sort of person you are, my mistake I ever   255
married you. You've always had a hard day. / You
think I don't have a hard day? Lift wasn't

FRANK Yes I always have a hard day and who's it for?
Come back to this any wonder I don't come home?
Who has the money off me eh? Who has the money?   260

MARGARET working again for three hours, I put off going
to the shops then I had to go or they'd have shut, there
was no bread left, I carried the whole lot up the stairs
and the bag broke / the eggs fell out, there's no eggs
for breakfast you   265

FRANK It's your job. I don't moan. I get on with it, what's
wrong with this country nothing but moans, country
of old women.

MARGARET can do without, 32p the eggs, you've had your
  eggs in beer, you've had your kid's dinners and your   270
  kid's new shoes and your kid's school journey he can't
  go on because that would be a luxury / he don't need it
  like you need six pints.

FRANK Who earns it? Who earns it? Sooner I'm dead, then
  you'll see who earns the money, see what's what, see   275
  what it's like / managing on your own.

MARGARET Get a job myself, get a job up the school, school
  helper, could get that now / think I will,

FRANK What you get for that? Nothing.

MARGARET you can't support your family by yourself /   280
  better go out to work and help myself, enough of your
  talk.

FRANK Don't tell me I don't support my family, don't you
  say that. If my dad heard you say that, what he'd do if
  my mum said that, don't you say I don't support my   285
  family. Who has the money off me? If you can't make
  it last that's your lookout, you buy the wrong stuff /
  you buy

MARGARET You give her money.

FRANK frozen food, my mum never let us go hungry,   290
  you're no good in the house, rotten housekeeper, you
  buy rubbish. If I give her money, if I lend her money
  it's my money to lend. She's a woman on her own
  bringing up a child, I'd expect to hear more human
  sympathy from you / always on about feelings, you got   295
  no feelings for other people, only got feelings for
  yourself.

MARGARET Not enough money for the school journey he
  could have gone to the sea and you give her money,
  your own kid, showing him up in front of his mates,   300
  your own kid and you give the money to her, give her
  the whole lot I should, give her the housekeeping and

let her cook our dinner / frozen food, you'll be lucky if
she can

FRANK You got no feelings, I don't want to talk to you. I   305
don't want to listen. I don't like you.

MARGARET see out past her eyelashes to cook a fishfinger.
[*Silence*]

FRANK I'm not very happy. Are you happy?

MARGARET No.

FRANK My fault, is it?   310

MARGARET I'm not saying it's your fault / but …

FRANK But.

MARGARET Come on, I don't want a row.

FRANK Who's starting a row?

MARGARET I can't even talk to you without you shouting at   315
me because /

FRANK Who's shouting?

MARGARET you're too pissed to have /

FRANK Who's pissed?

MARGARET a proper talk.   320

FRANK Eh, who's pissed?

MARGARET I'm not for one, I don't get to go out / it's you
goes out.

FRANK You want a drink? Do I stop you having a drink?
You can buy drink in the supermarket, is it my fault   325
you don't enjoy yourself / you make yourself a martyr,
if I take you down the pub

MARGARET Drink at home by myself, no thank you, old
lady with a gin bottle.

FRANK you don't enjoy it or you start chatting up Charlie   330
don't you, think I'm stupid, blame me for everything,
go on blame me, that's what I'm for / come home at
night so you've someone to moan at.

MARGARET I do have feelings, you wouldn't know, you're
never here, you don't know nothing about me, night   335
after night round with her or up the pub or out with

Charlie, wherever you are it's not here, that's all I
know, what am I doing sitting here waiting for you
night after night, never here when you're needed like
the time I had the miscarriage where were you? you   340
knew I'd started and you went to the pub and you
went to Charlie's / you're here for the fun but that's

FRANK Didn't know what was happening, did I?

MARGARET all, here for the beer, you did know what was
happening, you're a liar, you always was a liar, you   345
stopped out on purpose / you knew, you did

FRANK This is five years ago, do us a favour, this is five
years ago.

MARGARET know, could have died all you cared, I don't
care if it's ten years ago I'll never forgive you / and   350
every time you go out now I'm not

FRANK You don't want me. You don't want me.

MARGARET surprised, I think yeh yeh, that's him, off he
goes, selfish bugger / what do you expect what

FRANK If I could afford it, I'd leave you. If I could get a   355
place.

MARGARET are you surprised for, haven't you learnt yet
that's what he's like, think he loves you stupid / course
he don't. Why don't you go

FRANK If it wasn't for the money and the kids.   360

MARGARET and live with her, she's got a nice place. Don't
stay with me just to keep yourself in beer, go and live
with her, / see how you like it.

FRANK Don't want to live with her. I don't even like her,
don't know why I keep seeing her. I was round there   365
tonight / is it any wonder? First

MARGARET I knew you was.

FRANK time for a week, / I don't know.

MARGARET I'd like to put a brick through her window. I'd
like to go round with a gun and she opens   370

FRANK Stop talking stupid.

MARGARET the door and I shoot her in the stomach. If it wasn't for the kids I'd get a gun. I'd like to see her bleed. I'd like to stamp

FRANK Shut it. Shut it.   375

MARGARET on her face. She's not that pretty. / What

FRANK It's not her.

MARGARET you must think of me.

FRANK It's not you.

Two

[PETE *and* DAWN *are lying on the bed.*
A long silence.
PETE *asks* DAWN *if she's all right:*]

PETE Uyuh?

DAWN Mmm.

PETE Ah.

DAWN [*moans*] Ohhhhh.
　　　[*A short silence.*
　　　PETE *asks how* DAWN *is:*]

PETE Mm? Mmm?   5

DAWN Uh.
　　　[*A long silence.*
　　　PETE *puts out the light. He asks if it was all right to put*
　　　out the light:]

PETE Uh?
　　　[*Silence*]

DAWN Ohhhhh.
　　　[*Silence.*
　　　PETE *is comfortable:*]

PETE Ah.
　　　[*A long silence.*
　　　DAWN *wakes with a start:*]

DAWN Oh.   10

PETE Huh?

DAWN Ohhhhh.

PETE Mmmm?
　　　[*A long silence.*
　　　DAWN *moans,* PETE *acknowledges.*
　　　DAWN *is fed up with the night,* PETE *sees where things*
　　　have got to:]

DAWN Ohhhhh.

PETE Mmm. 15

DAWN Ugh.

PETE Uh huh.

[*A short silence*]

The plot of *Alien*◊ is very simple. You have a group of people and something nasty and one by one the nasty picks them off. If you're not going to see it I'll tell you 20 the story. Mm?

DAWN Mm.

PETE There's these people in a spaceship, right, and it's not like *Startrek* because the women wear dungarees and do proper work and there's a black guy and they 25 talk about their wages. So they get a signal there's something alive out in space and it's one of their rules they have to investigate anything that might be alive, so they go to see what it is, right, and a couple of them go poking about on this planet and it's like a weird 30 giant fossil and they find some kind of eggs, and go poking about, and then there's a horrible jump and this thing gets on to John Hurt's face. They let him back in the ship and this horrible thing's all over his face and how can they get it off, that's quite 35 unpleasant. Then it gets off itself and disappears and he gets better. And then there's the horrible bit everyone knows about where he's eating his dinner and it comes bursting out of his stomach and there's blood everywhere and it looks like a prick with teeth, a 40 real little monster, but it's worse in the stills than in the movie because it goes so fast you hardly ever see it. That's quite good, I like that, when you think they might have shown it you all the time and they don't.

[*DAWN puts the light on; PETE protests:*]

Errr. 45

DAWN I feel completely unreal.

82

[*Silence.*
DAWN gets up.]

PETE Uh?

[*Silence*]

I like movies where nothing much happens. Long
movies, you can just sit there and look at them. *The
Tree of Wooden Clogs*◊ is a long movie. I wished they   50
didn't have an interval.

[*A long silence*]

DAWN I don't know if I'm unreal or everything else, but
something is.

PETE Uh huh.

[*Silence.*
PETE gets a book and reads.
DAWN dials a number on the phone. There's no reply.]

DAWN I think I'm dead.   55

[*Silence*]

PETE We could have something to eat.

[*Silence.*
PETE goes on reading. He asks if she wants something to eat:]

PETE Mm?

DAWN Mm.

[*PETE goes out.*
*DAWN gets dressed, beautifully, in a dress. She sits on
the bed.*
*PETE comes back with tray of food including a loaf and
a knife.*]

PETE Ooh?

DAWN I thought I might go out.   60

PETE It is three in the morning.

DAWN Ah.

PETE Don't let me stop you.

DAWN Right.

[*PETE eats.*
DAWN doesn't eat much.]

PETE Then there's this creature you see loose in the   65
spaceship and it might take any shape and it might get
any one of them any time, and of course it does.
There's a lot of creeping about in the dark looking for
it and wondering when it's going to pounce and what
it's going to look like. If you're looking forward to   70
being frightened you can be frightened but a friend of
mine went to sleep because it was so dark.

> [*Silence.*
> *PETE eats.*
> *DAWN gets undressed.*
> *PETE asks if she wants any more food; she says no. He is*
> *pleased to eat it*:]

Uh?

DAWN Uhuh.

PETE Mmm.   75

> [*Silence*]

DAWN I'm frightened.

> [*Silence*]

PETE You'd think from those German movies that
Germans were always sitting about not doing too
much and staring into space and then whenever you
meet Germans they're not like that at all, they're very   80
adult. I suppose the movies seem quite different there.

> [*Silence*]

I'm thinking of *The Left-handed Woman.*⋄ *The*
Goalkeeper's Fear of the Penalty.⋄ *The American*
Friend.⋄ No, there's more rushing about in *The*
American Friend. I won't tell you the plot, it's quite   85
confusing.

> [*Silence*]

DAWN I'm frightened.

> [*Silence.*
> *PETE finishes eating.*]

PETE The most frightening bit of *Alien* for me was when
one of the crew turns out to be a robot and his head
comes off.   90

[*Silence.*
PETE asks DAWN if she's all right:]

PETE Uyuh?

[*PETE puts some music on and goes to bed.*
DAWN phones again, again no reply.]

PETE I haven't seen my brother for two years. I haven't
seen my mother for five years. I haven't seen my father
for ten years.

[*Silence. Music.*]

Redupers,° that's another German movie. It's short for   95
the all-round reduced personality. Did I see it with you?

[*Silence. Music.*
DAWN plays with the knife.]

DAWN There's a voice in my head, no there's not a voice in
my head, come on. *I* keep saying to myself in my head,
I want to be dead, I want to be dead, and I don't think
it's true.   100

[*Silence. Music.*]

PETE So eventually there's no one left except this girl and
she runs away up and down the spaceship a whole lot
of times. And she gets away in a little escape space ship
and thinks she's safe and of course the thing's in there
with her. And she's getting undressed, which I thought   105
was a bit unnecessary but I suppose it makes her more
vulnerable is the idea, and in the end she gets the door
open and it's sucked out into space. So she gets a good
night's sleep which is more than I can say for some
people.   110

[*DAWN takes the knife and gets into bed.*
PETE is getting sleepy. He's glad she has come to bed. He
asks if she's all right. She says yes. He settles down more
comfortably:]

85

Mmmm. Mmm?

DAWN Mm.

PETE Ahhhhh.

>[*Long silence. Music.*
>*They are lying back to back.*
>*Under the sheet DAWN cuts her wrist.*
>*PETE stirs:*]

DAWN Ah –

PETE Uh?   115

>[*Silence.*
>*Blood begins to come through the sheet.*
>*The music ends.*
>*PETE reaches out and puts out the light without seeing.*]

Three

[MARGARET *and* PETE]

MARGARET I was so insecure that was part of it.

PETE You had no life of your own.

MARGARET I was just his wife, I wasn't a person.

PETE You can't blame him though I mean.

MARGARET I don't. I don't any more. I'm sorry for him.   5

PETE Yes, I'm sorry for him.

MARGARET He's still drinking. He hasn't changed.

PETE You're the one who's changed.

MARGARET I've changed. I was just his wife before. I had
no life.   10

PETE You can't blame him. It's what you learn to be like.

MARGARET It's what you learn but you can change yourself.
I've changed myself.

PETE I'm not saying a man can't change.

MARGARET You've changed, you say you've changed.   15

PETE I have yes but I can see, as a man, what the problem
is for him.

MARGARET You're not like a man in some ways not like
what I think of a man when I think what's wrong with
men.   20

PETE I'm still a man. I've just changed.

MARGARET We've both changed.

PETE Yes.

MARGARET It was getting the job made the difference. If I'd
met you before I got the job I'd have got in a panic, I'd   25
have thought is he going to marry me or what, is he
going to be a father to my children, I couldn't just be
happy. When I decided to go for being a nursery

87

assistant and get some training, that was amazing for me to think I could get trained and do something. 30

PETE You can't, though, can you?

MARGARET No, I can't but that's the cuts.

PETE At least you know what you want to do.

MARGARET That's it, I've got some idea of myself. I used not to be a person. 35

PETE I think you're wonderful.

MARGARET When I saw him last week it was like seeing a ghost. It's better when the kids go round to him and I don't see him. It makes me feel like a ghost myself. It used to be so horrible, you can feel it in the air when 40 you meet. I don't want to be like that any more. You wouldn't have liked me.

PETE I would, I would have known.

MARGARET I was horrible.

PETE You were very insecure. 45

MARGARET I had no life of my own. I was just his wife.

PETE I was horrible. I could hardly speak. I couldn't talk to Dawn. You and I just lie here and talk but I'd got with Dawn so I didn't know what to say to her. And she couldn't talk. It was me killing her. If we'd stayed 50 together she'd be dead by now, she'd have done it in the end so it worked, she'd be dead. I was doing that.

MARGARET She was putting a lot of pressure on you.

PETE She was asking for help.

MARGARET You couldn't put the world right for her. 55

PETE I could have talked. I was out of touch with my feelings.

MARGARET You're not now.

PETE No, I'm different now and she's different. If I run into her now she's fine, chats away, we chat away 60 perfectly all right. I didn't want her depending on me like that, I couldn't put the world right for her, I

couldn't take the pressure. I hated London, I hated
what it was doing to the kids I taught, I could hardly
walk down the street let alone sort her out, I couldn't   65
take it.

MARGARET You needed someone less dependent.

PETE It was a very destructive relationship.

MARGARET You were out of touch with your feelings.

PETE I dream about her with that sheet covered in blood.   70

MARGARET We talk about them a lot.

PETE Of course we do.

MARGARET We say the same things over and over.

PETE I suppose we're bound to for a bit.

MARGARET Of course we are.   75

PETE We have learnt.

    [*Silence*]

MARGARET If I can't get the nursery training I'll have to do
something.

PETE Of course you will.

MARGARET You say of course I will but it's not that easy, I   80
can't even be a helper now they've cut the helpers. I
don't want to be at home all the time, I'm a bit
frightened of that. And I need money.

PETE You don't have to make a martyr of yourself with
the housework.   85

MARGARET I don't make a martyr.

PETE No.

MARGARET It just makes sense if I'm the one who's here
and you're at work.

PETE I can't help it. I cook.   90

MARGARET Of course you do and the kids are mine, the
mess is mine.

PETE Don't worry so much about money. I'm earning
money.

MARGARET That's your money.   95

PETE I want to go to sleep.

MARGARET Are you unhappy?

PETE I'm tired.

    [*PETE puts the light out. Silence.*]

The microchip can do a billion thought processes in a second.   100

MARGARET You can't get a speck of dust on it.

PETE When I'm out of work too I'll clean the floor.

MARGARET You can do it Saturday.

    [*Silence*]

When did you last see Dawn?

PETE Last week sometime.   105

MARGARET Which day?

PETE Wednesday, Tuesday.

MARGARET Where was it?

PETE She was in the pub dinner-time.

MARGARET Don't you have to be at school at dinner-time?   110

PETE No.

MARGARET I thought you did special football dinner-play.

    [*Silence*]

PETE You see Frank more than I see Dawn.

MARGARET I don't see Frank.

    [*Silence*]

MARGARET Everyone's going to have to have hobbies.   115

PETE Everyone's going to be on the dole.

MARGARET It's the future, you have to go forward.

PETE Who's going to make money out of it?

MARGARET Think of robots. Don't you like the thought of robots?   120

PETE You're very wide awake.

MARGARET Sorry.

PETE Sorry but I do have to get up in the morning.

    [*A long silence*]

I'm very wide awake now.

MARGARET Uh?   125

PETE Sorry.

MARGARET What?

PETE Sh.

MARGARET Mm.

    [Silence]

  Are you asleep?   130

PETE No.

MARGARET What's the matter?

PETE I'm worrying.

MARGARET What about?

PETE Fascists.   135

MARGARET What?

    [Silence]

  Is it us?

PETE What?

MARGARET You keep being unhappy.

PETE What makes you think it's us?   140

MARGARET You used to be happy.

PETE I'm happy about us.

MARGARET Then what's the matter?

    [Silence]

  What is it?

PETE I don't know.   145

MARGARET What sort of thing?

    [Silence]

  It's not surprising I think it's us. If you keep being
  unhappy and won't tell me. I can't help thinking when
  I'm on my own. I know I'll be better when I get a job. I
  don't like being on my own and I know your meetings   150
  are important but I get frightened in the evening when
  the kids are asleep, I think what have I done? You
  don't like me talking like this, I can't help it, I've no
  one else to talk to, sometimes I don't talk to anyone all
  day, I can't help it if I'm frightened.   155

PETE I'm going to put the light on.

    [PETE puts the light on]

MARGARET I don't want to say this but I worry about
Dawn. You keep seeing her, you say you run into her,
what you keep running into her for? If you're seeing
her why not say so, I don't mind, I'm just afraid you   160
might go back to her. I don't mind nothing if you tell
me, it's when you don't tell me I think you're hiding
something, I think you're seeing her and not telling me,
is that true? I don't like lies, I never did like lies, I
know I'm insecure and why shouldn't you see her,   165
sleep with her if you want to, you're perfectly free,
we're not married, I don't want to be married, never
again, I don't want me and Frank, I wasn't a person,
and you and Dawn, I don't want that, so what are you
doing? Night after night out at meetings, I know   170
they're important, I get frightened, what have I done, I
left him for you, what have I done to the kids, what's
happening, and are you always at a meeting or do you
see Dawn, is that stupid? I want to make you happy
and I can't and I get frightened and you've got to tell   175
me everything. I don't want to be like this, you've got
to help me, please say something.
    [*A long silence*]
PETE I don't know what to say.
MARGARET No.
PETE I'm not doing this deliberately. I've stopped being   180
like this.
MARGARET Yes.
PETE Are you definitely not going to see *Apocalypse
Now*?◊
MARGARET I don't like war films.   185
PETE There's this guy who's already a war veteran and
he's back in Vietnam, he's a wreck but he can't keep
away from it, and he's given a mission to go up the
river and find this colonel who's gone mad and kill
him, right.   190

MARGARET Right.

PETE So he goes on a boat up the river to find him. And
the main thing is these amazing set pieces of
destruction, it starts with a sort of still grey shot of the
jungle and it bursts into flames and the whole thing   195
looks stunning, planes coming over and things
exploding, and there's music. So he's going up the river
on this boat to find the mad colonel and kill him, or
maybe not kill him, he's sort of attracted by him and
we are, of course, because we know it's Marlon   200
Brando. And on the way the Americans are killing
everybody and there's a mad officer who gets his
soldiers to go surfing and on the boat they kill a girl
and rescue a puppy and the black kid on the boat gets
killed and it's a real nightmare and he goes on up the   205
river to find the colonel.

RESOURCE NOTES

Who has written these plays and why?

Caryl Churchill

Caryl Churchill is a leading playwright of her generation and one of the most acclaimed dramatists in contemporary British theatre. She writes about a broad range of political, historical and social areas, but the fact that she is a woman cannot help but influence the perspective she presents in a play. It is often assumed, perhaps because she is a woman, that she writes exclusively for women and about issues which concern only women. Certainly many of her plays focus on sexual politics and feminism, but she does not restrict herself to any particular type of drama or theme.

Churchill began writing plays in the late 1950s as a student at Oxford University, and most of her early work was performed by students. Having married and had children, Churchill turned to radio drama as a way of continuing with her work, and during the 1960s and early 1970s had several plays broadcast on BBC Radio 3, including *Lovesick* (1965), *Abortive* (1971) and *Not ... Not ... Not ... Not ... Not Enough Oxygen* (1971). In 1972 she began to write plays for television and at about the same time she wrote *Owners*, her first stage play to have a professional production, at the Royal Court Theatre Upstairs.

The Royal Court Theatre in London is noted for its interest in new playwriting, and Churchill has continued her association with this theatre ever since her first production there. From 1974–75 she was writer in residence, presenting *Objections to Sex and Violence* (1975), which was followed by *Traps* (1977). Two of her most commercially successful plays were first presented there, *Top Girls* (1982) and *Serious Money* (1987), both of which transferred to New York.

Churchill has always welcomed opportunities to work on collaborative projects, not only with actors and directors but also with artists who work in other media – choreographers, composers, designers. Some of her most exciting work has resulted from workshop experiences and experimental group projects. *A Light Shining in Buckinghamshire* (1976), *Cloud Nine* (1979), *Fen* (1983) and *A Mouthful of Birds* (1986) were all produced as part of a workshop process set up by the Joint Stock Theatre Company. *Vinegar Tom* (1976) was written as the result of a collaboration with Monstrous Regiment, a socialist/feminist theatre group. More recently, co-operation with a range of performance practitioners such as dancers and opera singers has resulted in multi-media work, e.g. *The Lives of the Great Poisoners* (1991) and *The Skriker* (1994).

Churchill is an innovative playwright who experiments with different forms of theatre and ways of writing which challenge our normal expectations of plays, and which offer actors exciting opportunities for experimenting with the roles they play.

Women in theatre

In the past, the work of women in theatre has been given far less significance than the work of their male counterparts. Plays by women have been left out of the theatrical canon or not mentioned in theatre histories, and women have often been represented in a very restricted and stereotypical way on stage. Their roles have tended to be subordinate to the male roles, taking less stage space and time. For significant periods of theatrical history, women were banned from the stage completely and their roles were acted by men. In the time of Shakespeare, it would have been thought immoral for any women to appear on the stage. Even in more recent times, actresses have been treated with suspicion, and have often been considered to be no more than prostitutes.

Although attitudes have changed, it is still the case that fewer plays are written by women than by men, that there are fewer roles for female performers than male and that there are fewer women in positions of authority, such as director and producer, in theatre than there are men.

✦ Activities

In pairs:

1 Draw up two lists: one of male and one of female playwrights whom you have heard of. You can include writers who work on television drama if you wish. What conclusions can you draw by comparing these lists?

2 Check through publishers' catalogues, bibliographies, TV listings, reference books and library shelves and catalogues to find the names and dates of as many women playwrights as you can and the names of some of the plays that they have written. Who were their male contemporaries?

3 Look at the cast lists of a play by Shakespeare, a play by a nineteenth-century playwright, e.g. Chekhov, and a modern play. Compare the number of male and female roles in each play. Check through the text to estimate the amount of time the women spend on stage and the number of lines they speak in comparison with the men. Make a summary of the conclusions you can draw from this.

4 Make a list of the reasons why you think women might have been poorly represented in the dramatic field in the past, using the following headings:
   - why there are so few women playwrights;
   - why women's roles are fewer and shorter than men's;
   - why women performing have been treated with suspicion.

Contemporary women's theatre

Since the development of the women's and feminist movements of the early 1970s, a small group of women playwrights have worked to make women and the issues which concern them more visible to both the theatre-going public and to TV audiences. Many of these playwrights have worked on the fringes of mainstream theatre in small performance spaces, although some have infiltrated the West End and the popular slots in TV drama. As feminist theatre was developing, many women writers focused upon issues which were important to women and reflected the female experience, for example childbirth, motherhood and inequality in the workplace. These were areas that had been ignored by male playwrights in the past and theatre offered opportunities for educating women about their rights and raising their awareness of their unwarranted subordinate position in society.

Now more women are writing drama on a broad range of political and social issues, using various genres from comedy to police series, from drama to soap opera. Their work is appealing to a broad spectrum of theatre and TV audiences. Nevertheless, the necessity to present women as positive and active remains one of the principal concerns of many female playwrights and so the search for appropriate forms for representing women continues. Although women writers no longer confine themselves to what might loosely be termed 'female issues', they inevitably present a women's perspective which for centuries has been absent. The woman's voice is just beginning to be heard in theatre.

✦ *Activities*

In groups:

1 Produce evidence from the texts to show that *The After-Dinner Joke* and *Three More Sleepless Nights* are plays written by a woman who is keen to inform and educate her audience about gender roles. Present this to the rest of the class.

2 Choose one of the shorter plays by a woman playwright from the selection in Further Reading on pages 126 to 128 and read it aloud between you. Identify the main areas that

the playwright was interested in exploring. Are these of particular interest to women?

Contextual information on the plays

The After-Dinner Joke and *Three More Sleepless Nights* were written within two years of each other at the end of the 1970s.

The After-Dinner Joke was presented as part of the 'Play for Today' series on BBC1. 'Play for Today' was a series of often controversial new plays written especially for TV. The play was broadcast on 14 February 1978.

Three More Sleepless Nights was first presented in June 1980 as a short lunch-time show at the Soho Poly Theatre, a small-scale, fringe theatre in London. It was directed by Les Waters, who had acted as assistant director on Churchill's previous play, *Cloud Nine*. He has directed many of her subsequent plays.

✦ *Activities*

1 In groups, discuss the following statements on whether the issues of the plays are still relevant today:
   - neither of these plays could have been written today because they are out-of-date;
   - charities play a different role now to that portrayed in *The After-Dinner Joke*;
   - relationships between men and women today are different from the male/female relationships in *Three More Sleepless Night*s.

2 Write a description of the contrasting couples you might use if you were writing *Three More Sleepless Nights* today.

━━━━━━━━━━━━━ ✦ ━━━━━━━━━━━━━

What type of plays are these?

Both of these plays might be seen to be making a social comment. However, Churchill uses very different dramatic **genres** and **media** to present her comments. One play is written for TV, a very popular form of entertainment, while the other is written for the theatre, which attracts a much smaller audience.

In TV, the presence of the camera acts as an intermediary between the performance and the audience. It is the camera which determines what we see and how we see it. Theatre performance is also framed, restricted by the limits of the performance space, but theatre directors do not have the same amount of control over what their audience perceives.

♦ *Activities*

1 List the ways in which watching TV is different from going to the theatre.
2 List the ways in which you expect a TV play to be different from a play in the theatre.

The After-Dinner Joke

Use of satire
The play takes a humorous look at the way in which charities operate, exposing them as political institutions despite attempts to present them as nonpolitical. The play might be described as satirical. **Satire** uses humour, wit and irony to present a critical point of view on a particular issue. It holds an idea up for ridicule, lampooning it until it is exposed as absurd.

✦ *Activities*
1 In groups, discuss the following, jotting down the main points:
   - Caryl Churchill states in her Introduction (on pages 5 and 6) that the title of the play, *The After-Dinner Joke*, comes from an Oxfam publication, *The After Dinner Joke Book*. Why might the play's title be called satirical?
   - Why is humour a particularly effective way of presenting a critical point of view on any subject?
2 In pairs:
a Make a list of the different kinds of humour that are used in the play; for example slapstick, verbal jokes, visual jokes, witty language, and the revealing of double standards.
b Choose three examples of what might be called satire and describe the satirical point that each is making.

✦ *Extension activities*
If you wish to examine the notion of satire further, here are some ideas for you to explore.
1 You might have come across other examples of TV satire. *Spitting Image* uses caricature-type puppets (like exaggerated cartoons) to poke fun at public figures. Watch an episode of *Spitting Image*.
a Make a list of all the different issues it makes fun of.

b Describe three different ways in which satire is used to make a critical point.

2 Jonathan Swift was a late-seventeenth- / early-eighteenth-century writer who attacked corruption and dishonesty through satire. *A Modest Proposal*, written in 1729, is sub-titled 'for preventing the Children of poor People in Ireland, from being a Burden to their Parents or Country; and for making them beneficial to the Publick'. In it Swift suggests that the children of poor women in Ireland should be fattened up and fed to the rich so that the poor and their children are no longer a burden on society. He uses black humour to present a savage attack on attitudes to the poor in Ireland.

Read a copy of the pamphlet and consider:

a What types of humour can you find in this piece of writing? Give some examples.

b What are the similarities between this piece and Churchill's play?

3 The novelist Charles Dickens was aiming to comment on the failings of society to care for its children in his novels such as *Great Expectations* and *Nicholas Nickleby*, while TV director Ken Loach was commenting upon poor housing conditions in his TV film *Cathy Come Home*. Like Churchill and Swift, they both wanted to be critical of society, but they chose different literary and TV forms.

a Read the first chapter of *Hard Times* by Dickens and compare the way in which he makes social comment with the way Churchill does in her play.

b What point is Dickens trying to get across to his readers?

c Which piece of writing is more effective in getting across its point? Why?

d Write the first scene of Churchill's play as if it were the opening of a Dickens novel.

e Watch a video of *Cathy Come Home*, and find a way to describe the type of film it is.

f Make a list of the different ways in which the film's makers show that they are being critical of housing policy.

g How does this method of criticising issues compare with Churchill's play and Dickens's *Hard Times*.

The medium and the message

One of the aims of the 'Play for Today' series was to make people think about the society in which they lived. We have far fewer one-off plays on TV today, but there are still several forms of drama which try to encourage people to think about important issues which affect our lives. Other familiar forms of TV drama are:

• soap opera;
• the drama series and serial;
• situation comedy.

✦ *Activities*

1 Find a way of defining the above forms of TV drama and give examples of each.

2 Give examples of the ways in which each of these types of drama has tackled social issues on the screen.

3 Choose a well-known TV soap opera, drama series or situation comedy and write a treatment for one episode of about twelve scenes, in which an important issue is explored by the characters and their situations. A **treatment** is a detailed scene-by-scene synopsis of what you would include in the drama. Each scene is given a heading and there is some indication of where it takes place. Say which characters are suffering the problem, how the people they meet react to the problem and how the story develops in the episode.

Three More Sleepless Nights

This is a **minimalist** play, a play which uses very few props, costume, scenery or actors. It is a short play, which uses the same structure – a couple in bed – for all three scenes, which are performed on the same set. The social comment is made through the similarities and differences, particularly in the use of language, between the three couples who occupy the bed.

✦ *Activities*

1 In groups, discuss the following:

a Churchill's target in *The After-Dinner Joke* is charities. What is her target in this play?

b Why does Churchill use only one set, even though the scenes are in different locations?

2 What are the differences between the ways in which Frank and Margaret communicate and the ways in which Pete and Dawn communicate?

a Make a list of words which describe the characteristics of each couple's conversation. It might be useful to use words which have opposite meanings, e.g. 'loud/quiet', 'aggressive/passive'.

b Are there words which would describe the characteristics of both sets of conversation? Give some examples.

c How does the way in which the two couples speak to each other tell us something more or something different from the actual words they use?

3 Is it possible to write the same story of *Three More Sleepless Nights* in a different form from the one that Churchill has chosen?

a Write an outline of the story in **six** sentences.

b Why did Caryl Churchill write *Three More Sleepless Nights* as a play and not as a short story?

✦ *Extension activities*

Harold Pinter is a playwright who uses dialogue to show the difficulties of communication. Although he uses the speech patterns of everyday life, with the pauses and long silences that everybody experiences in conversation, his characters struggle to make themselves understood. *The Birthday Party*, which was written in 1958, is about a rather unsociable man who lives in a boarding house where he is terrorised by two sinister men at his birthday party, which has been organised by his well-meaning landlady.

1 Read the first five pages of Pinter's play.
a List the ways in which the style of Pinter's play is similar to and different from *Three More Sleepless Nights*. Focus on:
   • the types of characters;
   • the use of dialogue;
   • the style of setting.
b Compare the relationship between Meg and Petey in *The Birthday Party* with the couples in *Three More Sleepless Nights*. How does Pinter tell the audience what their relationship is like?

Other contemporary writers like Samuel Beckett have written in a minimalist form. Caryl Churchill also uses sparse dialogue and setting in her play *Fen*.

2 Find copies of plays from several playwrights from different periods, for example Shakespeare, Chekhov, Brecht and a modern writer like Stoppard or Ayckbourn.
a Compare them with *Three More Sleepless Nights* under the following headings:
   • the cast lists: how do they differ in terms of the number of actors required, the gender balance and the information given on each character?
   • the settings: how much description of the set is given? How much detail is required in the set? How many props would you need to use?

- the stage directions: compare the style and quantity of stage directions in your texts. Why do you think some are more detailed than others?
- the number of scenes: list the scenes in each play and how many different locations are required.

b What conclusions do you draw about the type of text each is?

◆

How were these plays produced?

Most writers do not initiate work specifically for either theatre or television. Although a writer might have an idea for a new play, s/he would not normally produce a full script before that idea had been tested out on a producer, a director or a theatre company. Once the project looked feasible, the writer would then be **commissioned** to write the script. Alternatively, the initial idea might come from the producer who would assemble a team to work on the project, including a writer to produce the script. It is very difficult for writers to get unsolicited new work presented by either TV or the theatre these days.

The After-Dinner Joke

TV commissioning and scheduling

TV plays are presented as part of an organised schedule and must compete for an audience with programmes on other TV channels. Although various criteria are used to measure success, all TV programmes are at the mercy of the ratings, and if they do not achieve their target viewing figures they are taken off the air. At the same time, statutory authorities demand that certain broadcasting standards are maintained and a balance of programmes is presented.

The majority of dramatic writing for TV is required for soap operas and drama series, where scripts must adhere to a tightly controlled set of conditions, with each episode carefully planned by a production team before being handed over to the writer. Indeed, there are strict limits on the type of work that can be produced for most TV plays. Margaret Matheson decided on a theme which interested her as the producer of *Play for Today*, and Caryl Churchill's script was a response to that. The writer is only one of a large team making decisions about what should be included in any script. Also, programmes are restricted by their allotted time slot, which determines both their length and the time at which they will be broadcast. Bad language or excessive violence is not considered appropriate for screening before the 9.00 pm watershed. A strict budget is worked out for each project, limiting costs such as cast size, choice of location, costume expenditure and production time.

✦ *Activities*

1 Examine copies of TV listings publications, e.g. *Radio Times*, and work out where drama is placed in the schedules.
a From your research draw up a priority list of types of programme, including forms of dramatic fiction like films, soap operas, drama serials and one-off plays, as well as game shows, sport and news programmes.

b At what times of day is most drama shown? Why is this?

2 *The After-Dinner Joke* went out at 9.25 pm, after the News. Consider the audience for this play.

a Describe the type of audience you think the play is intended for. How did you arrive at your conclusions?

b Compare the popularity of one-off plays with other forms of drama on TV.

c Look at audience figures printed in newspapers or in TV listing publications and compare the popularity of drama with other types of programme, e.g. sport or game shows.

d Keep a record of your own viewing for one or two weeks and work out how much drama you watch. It might be interesting to ask someone in your family from a different generation to keep a record of their viewing for the same period of time and compare your viewing with the amount and type of drama that they watch.

e What conclusions can you draw?

Three More Sleepless Nights

The institution of theatre

Although theatre operates a commissioning system, Caryl Churchill wrote *Three More Sleepless Nights* as an **unsolicited** script. She was not asked in advance by a director or a theatre company to produce the work. She had just completed a very popular play, *Cloud Nine*, which established her reputation as a playwright, and therefore her work was in demand.

Although theatre puts more emphasis on the importance of the writer than TV does, there are considerable restrictions on the playwright. The final performance is a collaboration between the director, the performers, the designer and the writer. The play is limited by the policy of the theatre company and the amount of time, space and money available. The Soho Poly Theatre was a **fringe** theatre space with a low budget which presented plays at lunch time. Fringe theatre uses small spaces and has few expensive resources for productions. It is called 'fringe' theatre because it exists on the edges – the fringes – of the places where the big playhouses or **mainstream** theatre is located.

✦ *Activities*

1 List the ways in which a fringe theatre would be different to a large mainstream playhouse.
2 Choose one scene from *Three More Sleepless Nights* and re-write it as if it were to be presented at a large playhouse in a city, where they would have lots of technical resources. Think about how you would change the settings and the costumes, and add music and special effects. You can be as extravagant as you wish!

Collaborative working methods

Playwrights often work alone, completing a script for a company to work on before rehearsals begin. Sometimes, though, writers prefer to work with the actors before they write the script. Methods have been devised whereby the actors and directors are more involved in the process of creating the written material. Collective work of this kind can take several forms. Caryl Churchill has collaborated on four of her plays with a company called Joint Stock. This theatre group devised a system of producing new scripts where the performers and the director could have an input into the initial stages of the creative process, as well as being involved in the later stages of lifting the words off the page.

✦ *Activity*

a In pairs, choose a story from a newspaper and re-write it as a scene from a play. Adapt it freely to suit your own needs.
b With another pair, improvise short scenes which could follow on from each of the scenes produced in Activity **a**.
c By adapting and editing the improvisation, write your own polished version of the second scene so that it develops on from the first scene. Remember to think about the theatrical form you are using. Do you want your play to be funny or serious? Are you going to present it as documentary or satire, melodrama or tragedy?
d Compare your version with your original partner's.

The audience

Different plays and venues appeal to different types of audience, and theatre administrators must take account of the kind of audience they want to attract.

✦ *Activities*

1 What kind of audiences would you expect to see at the following:
  • a local arts centre;
  • a local repertory theatre;
  • a London musical;

- the National Theatre in London;
- an opera;
- a pantomime;
- a school play.

2 What kind of audience would you expect to visit the Soho Poly Theatre to see *Three More Sleepless Nights*? Give the reasons for your choice.

◆

How do the plays present their subjects?

The After-Dinner Joke

Naturalistic drama

Most TV drama is what is called **naturalistic**. It presents us with a recognisable world that resembles our own reality. It does not reproduce reality, but it does suggest that we are looking at a mirror of our own familiar world. *The After-Dinner Joke* is unusual for television in that it is not naturalistic. Nancy Banks-Smith, a television critic, said that it shows Selby '... as a sort of Alice in Charity Land. The electronic whizzery involved, colour separation overlay, gave it a particularly bright and paint-box look like a living strip cartoon or a Pollock's Toy Theatre' (*The Guardian*, 15 February 1978). In other words, it showed an artificial world of caricatures, rather than anywhere realistic.

As Nancy Banks-Smith suggests, the play takes the audience on a kind of journey of understanding.

✦ *Activities*

1 In groups, discuss the role that Selby plays on this 'journey'. Then, read Scene 10, where Selby meets Bruce Wingfield, and Scene 59, where she talks to a journalist.

a What is different about the way she perceives charities in the two scenes?

b What has made her change her point of view?

c Nominate the scene you think is most effective in showing that charities are political. Explain your choice to the rest of the class.

d Explain why you think the play ends in the way it does.

2 The scenes in the play are often short because in TV it is possible to change location very quickly. Throughout the play there are several types of scene which recur.

a In groups, discuss the purpose of the scenes in which Selby talks to the mayor.

b In pairs, read Scene 18, where a shoe is swapped for a fishing boat, and Scene 24, where calves are delivered instead of a car. Work out how an earlier episode in the play tells us what these scenes mean.

c Write a very short scene of your own that would work in the same way as one of these episodes.

3 On page 100 you were asked to compare the characters with the puppets in *Spitting Image*. They are not believable characters but are like cardboard cut-outs, or cartoon figures.

a Choose **two** of the characters in the play and describe how you would present them visually if you were the director and wanted them to look similar to the puppets in *Spitting Image*. A drawing could be used to illustrate your ideas.

b Why do you think that some of the characters in the play are known by their role or job, rather than by a name?

4 Television is a visual medium. In this play, the dialogue is kept to a minimum but it is set against strong images.

a In groups, act out Scene 48, the silent movie scene. Find ways of using the melodramatic form to make political points. The captions might be a useful device.

b Describe the difference between the style of acting in this scene and that in the rest of the play.

From page to screen

Before a script can be shot by the cameras, it needs to go through several stages. First of all a **storyboard** is produced. A storyboard is a pictorial representation of each shot of the play, presented like a comic strip. It is divided into scenes.

✦ *Activity: producing a storyboard*

Storyboarding can be a useful exercise for all kinds of story-telling: fiction, playwrighting, scripting films, etc. It encourages the writers to be clear about the way they construct episodes. Look at the opening scene of *The After-Dinner Joke*.

1 Prepare your own storyboard using the following instructions:

1	2	3	4

a Divide your paper into squares and number each square, as shown.

b Draw in each square the shots you would use if you were filming the script. You do not need to be a good artist for this exercise. Simple diagrammatic sketches are best. You might like to write a title under each picture, e.g. 'Price is sitting behind a large desk.' You need to make it clear whether you require:

• a **CU** or **close-up shot**, i.e. a shot that picks up a single item like a face, a door handle or a cup;

• an **MS** or **mid** or **medium shot**, i.e. a shot which shows the body from the waist to just above the head;

• an **MLS** or **medium long shot**, i.e. a shot that shows the whole figure, or part of the scene;

• an **LS** or **long shot**, i.e. a shot that shows the whole scene.

2 The information in the storyboard now needs to be extended and transferred onto a **shooting script**. This is a fully detailed script giving all the information required by the director, the camera-operator and the actor.

a Either type or hand-write the first scene on the right-hand side of the page only. Include information such as whether this is an interior (**INT**) or exterior (**EXT**) scene, the entry and exit of characters, and sound effects, e.g. the shutting of a door. Sound effects are indicated by the letters **FX**.

b On the left-hand side of the page put all the instructions the director would write in for presenting the play on screen. You will have the use of three cameras. Here is a selection of more terms that will be useful. You may have come across others that you want to use:

- **CAM**: camera;
- **FADE IN (UP)**: the gradual appearance of the scene from nothing;
- **MIX** or **DISSOLVE**: the transition from one scene to the next by fading out the end of one scene while fading in the beginning of the following scene;
- **PAN**: to swing the camera from left to right or right to left;
- **TRACK**: to move the camera parallel to the action on a set of wheels or a track;
- **2-SHOT**: a shot covering two characters (a **3-SHOT** would cover three).

Here is an example of how you might begin:

	LEFT	RIGHT
1		SCENE 1: OPENING TITLES
		(FX: Opening Music)
2	MIX TO CAM 1	2. INT: PRICE'S OFFICE. DAY
	MLS–Price's Desk	PRICE is sitting behind a large desk;
		SELBY is standing in front of it
3	CAM 2	PRICE
	CU PRICE	Do I understand you are resigning,
		Miss Selby?
4	CAM 3	SELBY
	CU SELBY	I want to do good, Mr Price.

5	MIX TO CAM 1 2-shot	PRICE And you think that being personal secretary to my sales manager isn't doing good?
	hold 2-shot	SELBY No, sir.
		PRICE Perhaps you think my sales manager isn't doing good.

This is a very precise task which takes a long time. It is carried out by the director not the writer, but is fundamental to organising what the audience sees.

✦ Extension activity

If you have access to video equipment you might like to try shooting the scene, although you will need to edit the material before it is ready for viewing.

Three More Sleepless Nights

Text and meaning

The play focuses upon the repetitive patterns of existence within the lives of three couples. By comparing the ways in which these relationships correspond and differ, Churchill shows how difficult it is to change.

✦ *Activities*

1 Write a description of each of the two couples in Scenes 1 and 2, making the differences and similarities between their lives and outlooks clear. Write under headings such as 'Type of Living Accommodation', 'Preferred Forms of Entertainment', 'Size of Family', 'Type of Food Eaten', etc., to make the comparison obvious. You will have to make up some of the detail of their lives which is not given in the play.

2 In groups:

a Make a list of all the faults and misdeeds that Margaret and Frank accuse each other of. What do you make of this list?

b Find three examples of times when one or other of them tries to redirect an accusation.

c Read Scene 2 and discuss why Pete tells the story of films to Dawn.

d Write down all of Dawn's words (you can leave out the sounds she makes), and suggest what responses she wants from Pete.

3 In pairs, read Scene 3.

a What aspects at the beginning of this scene might be surprising to the audience?

b Jot down features of the language from Scenes 1 and 2 which reappear in Scene 3.

c Decide why you think Churchill makes Pete and Margaret return to the same pattern of talking you have seen earlier in the play. Explain your ideas to another pair.

4 Why do you think Churchill uses a bed as the place where discussion takes place, and not a kitchen table or a park bench? Choose one of the following similar situations:
- the meal table;
- the classroom;
- the work place.

a Write two short scenes with different characters in each scene, which are located in quite different places but which use the same set. You might like to try out some of the non-verbal sounds that Churchill uses in her Scene 2.

b Can you write a third scene which draws together characters and ideas from both scenes?

5 In pairs, read Scene 2 so that Pete says Dawn's lines and Dawn says Pete's.

a How does this challenge what we expect men and women to be like?

b How do you think the gender roles they play affect the lives of Frank and Margaret and Pete and Dawn?

6 *Three More Sleepless Nights* was the first play in which Caryl Churchill used overlapping dialogue, although it has now become a hallmark of her work.

a In pairs, read aloud the first scene of *Three More Sleepless Nights* making sure that you overlap the speeches as Churchill describes at the beginning of the play. This is very difficult and might take some time to perfect. Try out your reading on an audience of another pair.

b Write a short piece of dialogue overlapping the speech in the same way that Churchill does. With your partner, read this aloud to another pair or act out the scene to your class.

c In groups, read the opening scene of *Top Girls*, where this overlapping speech is extended to include more than two people. What adjustments does Churchill have to make to her system when a group of people are in a scene?

From page to stage

Caryl Churchill gives few stage directions in the text. She leaves those to the director and the actors.

✦ *Activities*

1 Imagine you are directing the play. Write out one page of the script on the left-hand side of your page. On the right-hand side, jot down all the directions you would use. Place them opposite the relevant dialogue. You should include instructions on where you would use music and changes in light, as well as gestures and movement. It might help if you use different coloured pens for the script and the instructions.

2 Sketch a design for the set of your production of the play. Remember it has to be minimalist, but you can be imaginative. Make it clear where you are seating your audience, for example all the way around the edge of the space, or at one end of it.

✦

Who reads/watches these plays?
How do they interpret them?

This book only allows you to read the written text of the plays. You have to imagine what the productions would be like on the TV or on the stage. Every play is written to be performed, and the performances are just as important as the texts. In the theatre many different versions of the play can be performed, but on TV there is usually only one version of the play.

The reading of a play

The **reading** of a play is not limited to understanding the words on the page. It is the overall interpretation of the text in performance by its director and its performers. The audience also works out its own reading as it interprets the play during a performance. Whatever the author intends, there are many different ways of interpreting a script, and every new production of a play text will present a new reading, depending on the director and performers.

Critics are a special type of audience who write about their interpretation of plays and performances, although you could be called a critic when you talk about your opinion of a play and the way it has been directed.

✦ *Activities*

1 In groups:
a Discuss why there are very few newspaper reviews of *The After-Dinner Joke* and *Three More Sleepless Nights*.
b Look at the theatre or TV criticism in two or three of this week's newspapers. Try to find criticisms of the same play and compare the different readings of the critics. The following headings might be useful:
   • the differences in the way they describe the play;
   • what they like and dislike about the play and the performance;

- whether they focus on the acting, the directing, the writing or the interpretation.

2 Choose a piece of TV drama you have seen recently and write your own critical review of it, making clear your reading of the performance.

The After-Dinner Joke

The director and the actors developed their own interpretation of the text of *The After-Dinner Joke* which was presented on TV. Caryl Churchill thinks that *The After-Dinner Joke* could be presented on the stage, but some adjustments would have to be made and a different reading would result.

✦ Activities

In groups:

1 Discuss what would be the main problems you would meet if you were to present this text on the stage. How would you overcome these?

2 Divide your group in two, and each half choose two or three of the following areas to work through. You will have to co-operate closely.

a Re-write sections to eliminate dated phrases.

b Go through the cast list and work out how you might double or triple roles (i.e. actors playing more than one role). Work out exactly how many men and how many women you would need for your production.

c Draw a diagram of the stage space you would use, indicating the shape of the space and where the audience would sit.

d Design a set for your production indicating how you would make clear to the audience what location the stage space represents at any moment. How would you change scenes?

e Decide how to costume the characters, particularly if you want to retain Churchill's use of cartoon-like characters. Draw two or three designs.

As a group, present your ideas for the production to the rest of the class, using diagrams to illustrate your interpretation. Compare the different readings of the play that are presented to the class by each group.

Three More Sleepless Nights

Your understanding or reading of a performance is often affected by what you know of the actors. Certain performers are associated with particular types of drama, for example there are actors who specialise in comedy and others who are seen more frequently in classic drama serials. Some actors surprise their audience by appearing in roles unusual for them.

✦ *Activities*

1 Imagine you were casting *Three More Sleepless Nights*.

a Who would you like to cast as the couples? You can use any actors who you know, including those on TV. You don't have to know their real names; the names of their TV characters will do. Explain your decisions.

b What effect on the reading of the play does your casting have?

2 Write down what you think Scene 2 is about. Then, in pairs:

a Read through the first part of Scene 2 aloud, working out how to make sense of the non-verbal sounds that Churchill writes. Find alternative interpretations for these sounds. You will find that your different interpretations of the sounds change the interpretation of the characters and therefore of the play.

b Read the rest of the scene carefully and discuss:
   • who you think Dawn is ringing and why;
   • why you think she gets dressed and what sort of clothes she puts on;
   • why she cuts her wrist.

c Rehearse with your partner a way of dramatising this scene to show the underlying reasons for Dawn's behaviour.

d Show your scene to another pair in the class and then watch their interpretation of the scene.

e Compare your different readings and the ways in which you chose to dramatise this for your audience.

3 Look at your original interpretation of the scene (question 2) and consider whether your reading of the play has changed during your rehearsal of the scene.

◆

GLOSSARY

The After-Dinner Joke

14 **Ted Heath:** leader of the Conservative Party from 1965 to 1975, and Prime Minister from 1970 to 1974. An accomplished musician.

14 **Margaret Thatcher:** leader of the Conservative Party from 1975 to 1990, and Prime Minister from 1979 to 1990.

14 **jubilee:** the twenty-fifth anniversary of the Queen's accession to the throne was celebrated with a jubilee in 1977.

17 **lib-lab:** the Lib-Lab pact was an alliance between the Liberal and Labour Parties between 1974 and 1979, which ensured that Labour could hold onto government while having a narrow majority in parliament.

32 **Imperial Tobacco:** a cigarette producing company.

39 **Windscale:** now known as Sellafield, a nuclear reprocessing plant.

43 **Unilever:** a multinational corporation, known for producing cleaning products.

48 **Oman:** an oil-rich Sultanate state in the Middle East, linked by treaty with Britain.

Three More Sleepless Nights

82 **Alien:** US film directed by Ridley Scott in 1979.

83 **The Tree of Wooden Clogs:** Italian film directed by Ermanno Olmi in 1978.

84 **The Left-handed Woman:** German film directed by Peter Handke in 1977.

84 **The Goalkeeper's Fear of the Penalty:** German film directed by Wim Wenders in 1977.

84 **The American Friend:** German film directed by Wim Wenders in 1977.

85 **Redupers:** German film directed by Helke Sander in 1977.

92 **Apocalypse Now:** US film directed by Francis Coppola in 1979.

FURTHER READING

Other plays by Caryl Churchill

Light Shining in Buckinghamshire (Nick Hern Books, 1989)

Vinegar Tom (in Michelene Wandor (ed.), *Plays By Women: Volume One*, Methuen, 1982)

Cloud Nine (Nick Hern Books, 1989)

Top Girls (Methuen Student Edition, 1991)

Fen (in *Caryl Churchill: Plays Two*, Methuen, 1983)

Serious Money (in *Caryl Churchill: Plays Two*, Methuen, 1987)

The Skriker (Nick Hern Books, 1994)

Caryl Churchill: Plays One (Methuen, 1993: includes *Owners, Vinegar Tom, Traps, Light Shining in Buckinghamshire, Cloud Nine*)

Caryl Churchill: Plays Two (Methuen, 1993: includes *Softcops, Top Girls, Fen, Serious Money*)

Some plays by other women playwrights

Sarah Daniels, *Masterpieces* (Methuen, 1984)
                The Gut Girls (Methuen, 1989)

Shelagh Delaney, *A Taste of Honey* (Methuen, 1982: first performed in 1958)

Ann Devlin, *Ourselves Alone* (Faber, 1986)

Pam Gems, *Dusa, Fish, Stas, and Vi* (in Michelene Wandor (ed.), *Plays By Women: Volume One*, Methuen, 1982: first performed in 1976)

Debbie Horsfield, *The Red Devils Trilogy* (Methuen, 1986)

Charlotte Keatley, *My Mother Said I Never Should* (Methuen, 1988)

Sharman MacDonald, *When I Was A Girl I Used To Scream And Shout* (Faber, 1985)

Winsome Pinnock, *Leave Taking* (in Kate Harwood (ed.), *First Run*, Nick Hern Books, 1989)

Timberlake Wertenbaker, *Our Country's Good* (Methuen, 1988)

The Love of the Nightingale (Faber, 1989)

Olwen Wymark, *Find Me* (in Michelene Wandor (ed.), *Plays By Women: Volume Two*, Methuen, 1983: first performed in 1977)

A selection of critical books on Churchill

Geraldine Cousin, *Churchill the Playwright* (Methuen, 1989)

Linda Fitzsimmons, *File On Churchill* (Methuen, 1989)

Amelia Howe Kritzer, *The Plays of Caryl Churchill* (Macmillan, 1991)

A selection of critical books on women's theatre

(Most of these contain material on Churchill as well as other writers.)

Trevor R. Griffiths and Margaret Llewellyn Jones (eds), *British and Irish Women Dramatists since 1958* (Open University Press, 1993)

Helene Keyssar, *Feminist Theatre* (Macmillan, 1984)

Sue-Ellen Case, *Feminism and Theatre* (Macmillan, 1988)

Lizbeth Goodman, *Contemporary Feminist Theatres: to each her own* (Routledge, 1993)

Michelene Wandor, *Carry On Understudies: theatre and sexual politics* (Routledge, 1986)

A selection of books on television and TV drama

George Brandt (ed.), *British Television Drama* (Cambridge University Press, 1981)

David Self, *Television Drama: an introduction* (Macmillan, 1984)

John Fiske and John Hartley, *Reading Television* (Routledge, 1978)